TRAVELLING WITH KIDS TO DISNEYLAND PARIS

The guide to a magical family trip

Cristina Martínez Samalea

TRAVELLING WITH KIDS TO DISNEYLAND PARIS
2024 Edition

Cristina Martínez Samalea
cmsamalea@gmail.com
Instagram: Travelling_with_Kids_Guides

ISBN: 9798323592739

Part of the proceeds from this guide are allocated to the Juegaterapia Foundation and Aladina Foundation to support their projects in children's hospitals.

Copyright notice

Disclaimer of Warranty and Limit of Liability

To Rocío, Jorge, and Cristina, everything, always

Mum

Index

About Me

In the spring of 1994, my parents loaded their beloved Volvo with a bunch of suitcases and "just in case" stuff, and most importantly, with my three siblings and me, and set off for Euro Disney. Over 1,800 km and 3 days on the road, with four kids aged between two and eleven, would test anyone's patience, but that didn't stop them from giving us a magical experience, and the first big trip of our lives.

At that time, I was 8 years old, and my dreams were to become a Disney cartoonist and have 50 children - pretty average stuff! Luckily, over time, I reconsidered and settled for a healthy middle ground, with my three kids, Rocío, Jorge, and Cristina. For them, I draw tons of their favourite Disney characters, share this passion for the theme parks, and try to give them the magical childhood my parents gave me, with their enormous generosity and imagination.

This guide was born as a gift for my kids, which I gradually completed for my friends and family, until I decided to take the plunge and share it with you all. To be brief, these pages are dedicated to moms and dads, but of course I speak also to the most dedicated grandparents, the coolest uncle in the world (you've earned it), or the best (fairy) godmother. All of you who want to share this magical journey with the kids, or enjoy it like children!

In these pages, fully updated for the year 2024, you will find all the tips, tricks, and secrets to fill this journey with magic, not miss a single detail of the park, and make the most of your visit to Disneyland Paris.

Before the Trip

If this guide is in your hands, it means that you have already taken the first and most important step: planning the trip!

To make the most of a short but intense visit, it is best to arrange it in advance; Disneyland Paris is not a destination where last-minute plans work well, and information is power... magical power in this case!

Throughout this guide, you will discover all the secrets and stories of the park, which areas may interest you the most, the must-see attractions for everyone, itineraries, and strategies to save you time on those nerve cracking queues! You will become true "ninjas" of Disneyland Paris, and the kids will be amazed by all your tricks. In the words of Walt Disney himself, "there is no magic in magic, it's all in the details", and with these pages, you won't miss any of them.

Before we begin, consider some general advice. To stay informed about news, special events, or service interruptions (such as the strikes in June 2023), besides downloading the official park app, you can follow Disneyland Paris's official accounts on your social networks. Or even join Disney Facebook groups, which are full of information, recommendations, and options to share expenses with other travellers.

Budget wise, Disneyland Paris is not the most economical destination, but ticket and hotel prices vary greatly between high and mid-season, and depending on the proximity of the trip. Therefore, once again, it is advisable to book in advance and look for dates with lower attendance. You will also have plenty of accommodation and dining options to adjust your spending range to your budget.

As for the route through the parks, plan a more or less "linear" visit, seeing as much as possible of each area and park before moving on to the next, so you waste less time wandering. To do this, it is best to download the official app well before traveling and explore it, discovering the map and waiting times to plan your best route. In our "recommended itineraries" section, you will find examples of itineraries for one or two-day visits.

Your plans will probably change during the visit, depending on the weather, or if you want to ride an attraction you loved again, but with these tips, you will have a general idea of what interests you the most and won't waste time not knowing what to do. And, of course, if a highly demanded attraction has a short queue, head straight to it!

Prioritise and psychologize. Make a list of the "must-dos" for each family member, so you don't overwhelm yourselves trying to do everything but rather focus on what's most special for each one.

Also, you'll have to explain to the kids that the day goes by quickly and there may be queues and closed attractions. Don't promise what you will do or see (the weather may be bad, or Rapunzel might have stayed home untangling her hair), but what you "hope to do."

Prepare yourselves: the trip is tiring, as you will walk a lot, at least about 10 km per day, and even though you may not notice it in moments of excitement, you'll likely wake up with sore muscles the next day. If possible, "train" everyone a bit before the trip with some daily walks and weekend getaways to the countryside, to arrive in good shape and know in advance how far your children can walk without getting tired.

It's also good to know how well the little ones tolerate slightly more intense attractions. Both before and during the trip go "from less to more". For example, the Pirates of the Caribbean attraction has two "medium" drops; if they enjoy those, they can ride Star Tours or even Big Thunder Mountain. Similarly, if they are prone to motion sickness, you can avoid high speeds on the Teacups or carousels.

Before you go, measure the kids with the shoes they will wear and check which attractions they will be able to access. If your little one loves a bit of adrenaline but won't be able to get on certain rides, it's best that they know in advance. In our attraction chart, right at the end of the guide, you will see the height and age restrictions for each attraction; we have also put together nearby alternative plans, in case one of the kids cannot ride on one. Remember that children under 7 years old must be accompanied on all attractions.

Finally, arm yourselves with patience. Although in our heads in "the happiest place on Earth" kids are always happy, we have to be realistic: the power of magic is strong but not infallible! Of course, the trip will be full of excitement for them, but they are still our kids, who get tired on long days, who may want everything but can't have it all, and who will have tantrums and moments of boredom in queues.

Plan breaks and entertainment to avoid as many crises as possible, but if they happen, stay patient and calm, everything will pass! Although the trip may not be relaxing, it is very special, and will likely become a unique experience, and one of the best memories of their childhood.

Magic awaits you!

Introduction

Disneyland Paris is a holiday resort located in Marne-la-Vallée, a municipality about 50 km east of Paris. It comprises two adjacent theme parks:

- **Disneyland Park,** the most important one, and the first to be set in Paris, in 1992. It consists of 5 areas or "lands" dedicated to the great classics of the Disney universe, filled with attractions, restaurants, shows, and characters.

- **Walt Disney Studios:** opened in 2002, it is dedicated to the entertainment industry and themed as a huge film and animation studio. Currently, it has 4 "lands" or areas, and a large expansion will be added in 2024, completing its offering of attractions, theatres, and restaurants, surrounding a lake. To celebrate this new chapter, Walt Disney Studios Park will be renamed **Disney Adventure World.**

Additionally, the complex includes a dining and shopping area, Disney Village, open 24 hours, whose shops and restaurants have longer hours than the parks.

The resort is surrounded by a wide range of accommodation, both in Disney hotels and in partner hotels recommended by Disneyland Paris.

What is the best time to visit Disneyland Paris?

This is the key question and, in fact, it's a double one! On one hand, what is the best age to take your kids? And on the other one, what is the best time of the year to travel? Let's break it down!

At what age should you take the kids?

Disneyland Paris is a magical place for children... and not-so-children! There are attraction and show options for any visitor of any age and taste. Usually, families visit the park with children aged between 5 and 10 years old, when they don't get tired so easily, have fewer limitations to ride attractions, live the "Disney" magic with great excitement, and keep more memories of the trip.

That said, Disneyland Paris offers two children's discount brackets, which are worth considering:

- **Children under 3 years old**: they do not pay admission to the parks, accommodation in hotels, or meals if they share a menu at the restaurant. These conditions apply as long as the first day of the reservation is before their third birthday. Just before turning 3, they will enjoy the experience greatly, and although they won't have a clear and complete memory of the entire trip, you will be surprised by how much they remember everything that is not part of their usual routine.

  Our tips in the "Travelling with Babies" chapter will help make the experience as magical and comfortable as possible, for them and for you, including which attractions are more recommended at each moment. If you have a big family, also consider which hotels have rooms with capacity for more than 4 people (and a child under 3 years old). If you travel when your child is younger, you will save some money by not having to book two rooms, since you can request a crib for him for free.

- **Children from 3 to 11 years old** (inclusive): they qualify for the child rate, with significant discounts on tickets, accommodation, and meals. From the age of 12, you will have to pay the adult rate.

These discounts represent considerable savings in the total cost of the trip. Additionally, Disneyland Paris, more than a park with thrilling attractions, is a place to enjoy fantasy and the Disney universe, so it's better to go "sooner" rather than "later": your children will experience the park's magic more and your budget will appreciate it!

Throughout this guide, we will give you tricks to make the trip less tiring and manage the visit for the whole family (even if you are travelling with children of very different ages), so that, even if your children are very young, you can create unforgettable memories with them.

What is the best season to visit Disneyland Paris?

Choose wisely when to travel. This step is key to enjoying the park more, and for that, it is best to plan the trip in advance since it is not a destination where last-minute plans work well. Paris (and Disneyland) are the most visited places in Europe, and the pandemic forced many trips to be delayed. Since the restrictions were lifted, there is no longer a low attendance season, but rather high and medium ones, and the crowds vary significantly from season to season.

Travelling during peak times will considerably limit your visit as you will encounter long queues at attractions, restaurants, and shows. Additionally, high attendance not only increases queues at attractions but also the prices of tickets and accommodation. To adjust the trip budget, it is best to book in advance, during the low season, and, if possible, have flexible dates.

Prices no longer depend on exclusive or seasonal offers, they gradually increase, almost every day, as the date approaches and fewer rooms are available.

As for the total amount, although the cost of reservations varies by day on the official website, the months with the lowest prices are usually January and February, due to the temperatures, and French school holidays in this period spent practising winter sports. However, keep in mind that in these months the park closes much earlier, some days even at 6 p.m., which balances the price per time compared to other months: you will pay less but will be able to enjoy fewer hours per day.

With the arrival of spring, temperatures and attendance increase naturally. March is a good month to travel, cold but "bearable", with low attendance until Easter, and few bank holidays. In April, Easter Week and French school holidays increase attendance. In May, the weather is pleasant, and although it coincides with several French school holidays, the opening hours are extended until 10-11 p.m., so you will make the most of the time for rides, character encounters, or shows.

June is another great option, with very pleasant weather and medium attendance, both of which will grow exponentially during the months of July and August.

Travelling in September is a good choice, with mild temperatures and no French school holidays. Low attendance will continue during the first two weeks of October, but starting on October 1st, the Halloween season begins, which, combined with French school holidays, will fill the park with decorations and exclusive events, but also visitors. This high attendance will decrease in mid-November and will increase again during the Christmas season.

Think about what the family's priorities are: whether it's making the most of the budget, enjoying the trip at a special time (such as a family celebration or a thematic season), taking advantage of the school holidays in your country, or being able to see all the shows and attractions. Depending on these priorities, each time of the year has its own advantages and disadvantages, which we will try to summarise in the following table.

What is the best time to visit Disneyland Paris?

Month	Crowd Calendar	Weather	Seasons and events	French school holidays	France public holidays
January	Less busy				1/01/2025 - New Year's Day
February	Less busy		Chinese New Year and St. Valentine's Day	Winter holidays 08/02/2025 - 10/03/2025	
March	Less busy		St. Patrick's Day		
April	Busy			Spring holidays 05/04/2025- 05/05/2025	21/04/2024 - Easter Monday
May	Busy		May the 4th - Star Wars Day	Ascension holidays 30/05/2025- 02/06/2025	1/05/2025 - Labour Day 8/05/2025 - Victory 1945 29/05/2024 - Ascension Day
June	Busiest		June the 17th - Disneyland Pride		
July	Busiest			Summer holidays 05/07/2025- 01/09/2025	14/07/2025 - National Day
August	Busiest				15/08/2025 - Assumption of Mary
September	Busy				
October	Busy		Halloween 1/10/2024- 03/11/2024		
November	Busy				1/11/2024 - All Saints' Day 11/11/2024 - Armistice Day
December	Busiest		Christmas 09/11/2024- 06/01/2025	Xmas Holidays 21/12/2024 - 06/01/2025	25/12/2024 - Christmas Day

Weather at Disneyland Paris

In Paris, the climate is mild, compared to other European countries, without extreme temperatures, although with abundant rain and cloudy days.

Summer is short and pleasant, with temperature peaks around 30°C/86°F, except for occasional heat waves in July and August, the hottest months.

In autumn temperatures gradually drop, ranging between 5°C/41°F and 10°C/50°F. October and November are windy and cloudy, with abundant rainfall.

Winter is long and cold, with lows around 0°C/32°F that can drop even lower during polar cold waves. Although it's not a Nordic climate, you'll spend many hours outdoors in the park and it's wise to be prepared. In our "Travelling in bad weather" section, you'll find all the tips to enjoy the park in the middle of winter.

Spring is very pleasant. Minimum temperatures rise from around 5°C/41°F in March to 12°C/54°F in May, as well as maximum temperatures, from 10°C to 20°C (50-68°F); a perfect season for your visit.

Rain in Paris, both in spring and in the other seasons, is usually… unpredictable! Check the weather forecast in the days before your visit to adapt your luggage and plans to the ever-changing Paris skies.

Public Holidays and School Vacations in France

Although the entire complex is open 365 days a year, it's best to avoid bank holidays, and school vacations; especially French ones, which always increase attendance and prices, as about half of the visitors are nationals.

You may wonder why France has so many holidays. This is because France is divided into three zones for taking vacations in turns, so that the country doesn't collapse (including Disneyland Paris) and to reduce traffic jams. Therefore, the chart above includes from the first day of vacation in the first zone to the last day of vacation in the third one, for 2024 (if you can't avoid them, try not to coincide with those in zone C, which corresponds to Paris).

Additionally, keep in mind that in the French educational system, Wednesdays are off for children in elementary school, so many parents choose to go to the park with them on that free day. It's best to avoid it, especially in Disneyland Park, or make it a day to repeat the attractions you liked the most.

Celebrations and News at Disneyland Paris 2024

2024-25 will be a year full of news at Disneyland Paris. Throughout this year, several renovations and expansions initiated after the pandemic will be completed, and a new set of shows will be launched.

One of the main novelties of 2024 has been the reopening of the **Disneyland Hotel,** completely renovated, where its guests and visitors will experience the most exclusive experience in the "Princess Hotel."

On January 8, a new night time show on Sleeping Beauty Castle debuted, **"Disney Electrical Sky Parade"**, which will illuminate the park at night before the fireworks show, until January 6, 2025.

Until September 30, the park will also host **"A Million Splashes of Colour",** a musical parade of fantasy carriages with several daily passes in front of the Castle. You can find more details about both shows in our Show section.

Disneyland Park has also added new scenes and adventures to the rides "**Star Tours**" and "**Le Pays des Contes de Fées**".

Furthermore, in the sping of 2024, a new musical show full of surprises premiered at Walt Disney Studios. It is a brand-new show based on Wonderland universe, called **"Alice & the Queen of Hearts: Back to Wonderland"**, and is located right in the space where the stunts' show used to take place.

The park usually celebrates new Disney movies and series with exclusive merchandise, commemorative snacks or sweets, additional character encounters, nods in parades, or events around the attractions inspired by them. Thus, special activities related to the premieres of Elio (, Moana 2, Snow White and Mufasa, are expected during 2024.

On the other hand, until the pandemic, there were themed seasons, such as the Princess and Pirates Festival, Star Wars Season of the Force, or The Lion King Festival; celebrations that are expected to return in the future.

Currently, there are two main themed seasons, **Halloween** and **Christmas**. During Halloween festivities (dates are still pending confirmation), the park is filled with decoration, with jolly pumpkins and ghosts invading Main Street and Frontierland, exclusive "Meet and Greet" encounters, and special costumes for some characters.

Additionally, there is a specially themed parade, a show featuring the most famous villains, and, as a finale, a special experience on October 31.

Christmas is felt throughout the park between November and January, with festive decoration, Christmas merchandise, a special theme for the parade and fireworks, and exclusive visits from Santa Claus and Disney characters dressed for Christmas. On December 31, a "special experience" will be added to the park.

Finally, it's worth keeping an eye on the news regarding the new expansion of **Walt Disney Studios**, with a new lake and a huge Frozen-themed area, expected for 2025, and a new land based on The Lion King, that will open in 2026. As said, as a celebration of the opening of this "World of Frozen" and the renovation the Stuidio 1, the whole park will be renamed **"Disney Adventure World"**. Works on different areas are well advanced, such as the Rapunzel attraction, following the concept of the Mad Hatter's Teacups, under a beautiful dome with the magical atmosphere of Tangled.

How many days are needed to visit Disneyland Paris?

This question is linked to the previous ones, and the answer is, it depends! In the medium season, 3 full days may be enough, dedicating two days to Disneyland Park and its five territories or "lands," and one day to Walt Disney Studios and its four areas (although you may want to schedule some more time in case of bad weather).

During high attendance periods, the queues and crowds will make your visit much slower, and you will need at least 4 full days to see everything in both parks, ride most of the attractions, and eat peacefully. If you're travelling with babies, due to meal and nap times, and shifts for caring for them while the rest of the family is riding attractions, you'll need at least half an extra day.

The ideal is to arrive on Sunday afternoon (when many families are already going home) or Monday, and stay until Wednesday or Thursday, avoiding weekend traffic.

In our "Recommended Itineraries" section, you'll find tips to make the most of your visit to the park, depending on the number of travel days (even if you're only going for one or two days), and not miss the essential attractions and shows.

Planning to stay longer? Don't worry, there's always something to do in the park, not only can you repeat attractions and discover special spots, you may also enjoy hotel activities (especially if you're staying at Villages Nature) or visit Paris.

Park Hours and Extra Magic Time

Both Disneyland Park and Walt Disney Studios are open 365 days a year. The opening hours of both parks vary depending on the season and are always updated in the official Disneyland Paris App:

- In spring and summer, the parks open at 9:30 am and close at 10 - 11 pm, after the fireworks show.

- In autumn and winter, they also open at 9:30 am but close earlier, around 7 - 8 pm, advancing the night time shows.

While the official opening time is at 9:30 am, the parks generally open between 15 and 20 minutes earlier, so early risers can start heading to the first Land they want to visit (a strategy known as "rope dropping"), take photos with fewer people at the Castle, visit shops, or see characters on Main Street.

The opening hours of the attractions are the same as those of the park, with the exception of those that open early during Extra Magic Time, as you will see in the following section.

Regarding closing time, park hours are often extended on special festivities and weekends to balance larger crowds; and Walt Disney Studios usually closes an hour earlier than Disneyland Park.

Additionally, some attractions close a little earlier than others. However, if you're still in line at closing time, they'll allow you to access the attraction.

- In Disneyland Park, due to the parade, Main Street Vehicles and the Horse-Drawn Vehicles close in the early afternoon, as the parade goes through Main Street.

- Thunder Mesa Riverboat Landing, Casey Jr. Circus Train, and Le Pays des Contes de Fées close in the late afternoon.

- All Fantasyland attractions, as well as La Tanière du Dragon, close 1 hour before park closing, as this is the area used for the fireworks show.

Extra Magic Time (E.M.T.) or Extra Magic Hours

Guests staying at Disney hotels, as well as Gold annual pass holders, are allowed to access the parks one hour before the official opening time. If the parks open at their usual time of 9:30 a.m., Disney hotel guests can access from 8:30 a.m., gaining an hour of low-traffic visit. For this, the park gates open around 8:00 a.m., and hotel guests can access Main Street (a good time for photos, a coffee, etc.) until 8:30 a.m., when the Extra Magic Time attractions begin to open.

Not all park attractions open during this EMT, but some very popular ones do, such as Peter Pan's Flight or Big Thunder Mountain. Check which ones will be available in our "Lands and Attractions" table.

One last trick for an early entry is to book the first character breakfast slot at Plaza Gardens restaurant or at Auberge de Cendrillon, as you will see in our Restaurants section, to enter the park a little before 8 a.m.

How to book your tickets?

Park tickets are only sold online, they are not available at the ticket offices (except for visitors with disabilities). You can make your reservation through the official **Disneyland Paris website**.

www.disneylandparis.com

Before you start, we have a couple of tips. When researching ticket prices, accommodation, or flights, use the "incognito" or "private" mode of your browser so that subsequent searches do not increase the final price of your trip.

We also recommend comparing if there is a price variation between the different park pages, depending on the language. For example, sometimes the French website shows discounts or offers that are not on other websites.

If this happens, call Customer Service to apply for the French offer, or book directly through that site (although you will receive notifications in French, if the savings are significant, there is nothing that Google Translate cannot fix).

To solve any doubts about offers or during the booking process, Disneyland Paris has a Customer Service phone line, with a local call rate, depending on the country. Beware, as the lines are often busy and the waiting and processing time can be extended.

To avoid surprises on your phone bill, one trick is to contact Disneyland Paris through their official Facebook; they have a chatbot via private message where you can ask questions or request to be connected to a Disney agent. Another option to reduce the cost of the call is to use Google Voice or Skype, and call from a computer or smartphone. With the minimum credit, you will have more than enough minutes for your queries, and much more cost effective than phone calls.

By making the reservation yourself on the official Disneyland Paris website, you will save time and money, your tickets will be 100% official and secure, and you will receive the reservation information by email.

In fact, according to their "best price guaranteed" policy, if you find the same Hotel + Tickets package at a lower price up to a week after booking with Disneyland Paris, they will refund the difference and give you a voucher to use in the park's shops and restaurants.

Additionally, with your reservation, you will receive a free subscription to Disney+, and you will be able to link your reservations in the Disneyland Paris App, have all the information about your trip available and include your restaurant reservations and Premier Access through the App.

However, if you prefer the convenience of having an agency handle your reservation, there are many companies that offer complete travel packages and also allow for deferred payments, as well as cancellation insurance that covers the entire trip (stay, tickets, and flights). You can even take advantage of cashback pages to get a small refund of your expenses.

Finally, if you only want to book tickets, don't forget to check the private sales on websites like Vente Privée, Showroom Privé, etc., which occasionally offer ticket packages with significant discounts.

Steps to book on the official website

First, go to the Disneyland Paris website, and select the type of purchase you want to make: book only the tickets, or the standard package of tickets + hotel (Disney hotel or partner hotel).

Reservation of tickets + hotel

The official website offers hotel + ticket packages to the parks, not only in official Disney hotels but also in associated hotels (accommodations with a collaboration agreement with Disney).

You just have to access the corresponding section on the website under "Book your trip", select the arrival and departure dates, and the number of adults and children travelling. You can choose the hotel if you are looking for a specific one, or check the prices and availability of all of them.

In our **"Accommodation"** section, you will see the advantages and disadvantages of Disney hotels compared to partner hotels, and a brief summary of each of them. Consider the price, the distance to the park, whether you need to bring your own vehicle, and the room capacity, as you may need family rooms or connected single rooms.

If you have flexibility in dates, check the alternatives, as prices can vary by hundreds of euros from one week to another. The arrival date (if it is in high or low season) sets the price for the entire stay; it is important to choose it carefully.

Your standard package will include tickets to both parks for the same number of nights as your reservation, plus one extra day. This means that you can enter both parks from the day of your arrival until the day of departure, both included; with the exception of the Villages Nature resort, which only offers 2 days tickets. A trick to make the most of your time on the day of arrival is to book the previous night in an independent nearby hotel and enter the park the next day early morning.

Next, the website will ask you if you also want to book the **flight** to Paris. We recommend booking flights on your own to take advantage of other benefits, such as price comparison sites, air miles, cashback pages, etc. Some airlines, such as Iberia, offer packages including flights, park tickets and accommodation.

The next step is to choose whether you want to book only accommodation and tickets, or add a **Meal Plan** to your Disney hotel reservation. Meal Plans are packages with different offers to add meal vouchers to your stay. They are only available to Disney hotel guests and can be purchased at this step or added later; up to a week before your trip. In our "Meal Plans" chapter, we have prepared a summary of them, the types and modalities that exist, and when it is worthwhile to sign for them.

Next, both at the time of booking and later on, you can add **"extras"** to your reservation, such as a meal with characters or princesses, fast access to attractions (Disney Premier Access), or a flat-rate for photographs (Photopass). You will find all the details of these "extras" throughout this guide.

You can also add a **transfer from the airport** to Disneyland Paris and back with Magical Shuttle or the **Disney Express luggage service**, which will transfer your luggage from the station to the hotel, so you can speed up your arrival at the park.

In the next step, the website will show you a summary of your reservation, where you can add the names of the people who are part of your trip, include insurance, and check all the details.

Finally, you will proceed to **pay for your reservation**. A significant new feature of Disneyland Paris, which until now was only offered by agencies, is the possibility of paying for the trip in instalments, in a flexible, secure, and free way. You will pay a deposit of 15% of the total amount at the time of booking, and you can pay the rest in up to 5 instalments and up to 10 days before your arrival, through the website. Thanks to the current cancellation and modification policies, you can **cancel or modify** the reservation up to 7 days before the trip, receiving a full refund.

Reservation of tickets without hotel

If you decide to book tickets without the hotel, you can choose between:

- Visiting **both parks or just one**, in this case saving some money.

- Buying tickets with either **assigned dates or flexible dates**. To control the daily capacity, before the visit, the park requires you to register your tickets on the website for the selected date. In the case of tickets without an assigned date or annual passes; this should be done well in advance if you plan to travel in the high season. Keep in mind that the park fills up quickly on high demand dates. If your tickets are part of a Hotel + tickets package booked through the official website, this step is already done by Disneyland Paris.

In general, the ticket offering on the official website is usually the most cost effective in terms of prices and conditions, but every now and then ticket packages at an economical price appear on discount websites such as Attraction Tickets, Vente Privée, and Showroom Privée, or with added benefits on Booking.

Modifications and Cancellations

One of the lessons from the post-pandemic era is that any travel plan can go awry, and Disneyland Paris has learned from this: it currently allows you to **cancel or modify** your hotel + ticket reservation up to 7 days before arrival, obtaining a **full refund.** You also have the right to have the cost adjusted if the package price decreases due to a reduction in fees. Additionally, dated tickets can be cancelled up to 3 days before arrival, and undated tickets are valid for a whole year. To extend coverage for the last 7 days before arrival, include flights, or add medical assistance, you can purchase travel insurance from specialised companies such as Mondo, Iati, or Mapfre.

Claims and Complaints

A trip to Disneyland is a once-in-a-lifetime experience for many, a dream for almost every child, and for many parents as well; and obviously, a trip with a high cost. Therefore, if something does not meet your expectations, do not hesitate to kindly inform the Cast Members at the attraction or restaurant. The team's job is to make your stay enjoyable, and in many cases, they can improve the situation, provide explanations, arrange a table change, or resolve problems.

If you are still not satisfied with the solution provided, you can go to the Guest Relation Centers: City Hall in Disneyland Park, and Studio Services in Walt Disney Studios. If the issue is related to a Disney hotel, it is best to go directly to reception or call from your room. You can also file a complaint on the website by emailing park's Guest Relations Department at dlp.guest.communication@disneylandparis.com, or through an online form available on the park's website.

In any case, Disneyland Paris will attempt to provide you with a response, and if the complaint is upheld (as in the case of inconveniences caused by the strikes in June 2023), they will offer compensation, which varies depending on the loss caused (vouchers for shops, meal vouchers, additional tickets, or even partial refunds).

Discounts and Reduced Rates

In addition to reduced rates for children under 12, and free tickets and accommodation for children under 3, there are other discounts worth considering.

Disneyland Paris Annual Passes

If you plan to visit the park several times a year and will not be staying at a Disney hotel (which would include tickets), you may want to consider purchasing an **annual pass.** There are three types of passes: Bronze, Silver, and Gold. Prices range from €289/year (Bronze Pass) to €699/year (Gold Pass), and allow access during periods ranging from 170 days a year (Bronze) to 365 days (Gold).

They also include free parking, additional discounts on shopping and dining, and exclusive products and events for sale. It is worth considering their cost effectiveness in each case due to the high price and access limitations (for example, a Bronze pass does not allow you to reserve the second consecutive access day in advance).

At the time of the opening of sales for these passes, current Annual Pass holders and those renewing them will have priority for the new Disneyland Annual Pass program. These can be paid at once or in monthly instalments, and their food and shopping discounts may be valid for up to 6 people.

Military Discounts

At Disneyland Paris, a discount is applied for military personnel and up to 4 companions, on 2-day tickets without an associated accommodation package. To book these tickets, you must create an account and submit a valid military ID to certify your status, which you will need to bring to the park during your visit. This discount is subject to changes and modifications, and, although currently only military IDs from the United States, the United Kingdom, and France are accepted on the website, it is expected that military IDs from other nationalities will soon be incorporated.

Shareholders Club

Until 2017, individuals could buy shares of the Walt Disney Company and become members of the Shareholders Club, with small benefits on their visits, such as discounts on tickets and purchases, and access to the Salon Mickey Lounge, a small café inside the park. Since the majority of shares were repurchased by the company itself, the Club only offers its benefits to people who held the titles in 2017 and will close in 2027.

How to Get to Disneyland Paris

By Plane: Booking Flights

In general, it's more advantageous to book flights or other transportation on your own, using flight comparison websites such as Edreams, Skyscanner, or Booking, as well as the airlines' own websites. Besides ensuring the best price, you can also use your air miles, Travel Club points, OneWorld / British Airways Avios, and other reward programs.

There are also cashback websites that refund a percentage of expenses when accessing price-comparison portals through them. Although the earnings are minimal and vary depending on the company, it can be a pleasant surprise a few days after booking your flights.

Consider also purchasing **cancellation insurance** for flights. In recent years, changes to bookings due to personal circumstances or illness have increased, and you'll be covered if any eventuality occurs. Also, remember to check in for your flights as early as possible, both outbound and return.

Regarding the airports of origin, it's best to make as few layovers as possible, as they are twice as inconvenient when travelling with children. Take advantage of the **airport facilities for families,** from the exclusive security checkpoint for travellers with children and babies (faster and with simpler checks for liquids and baby food) to priority boarding queues and play areas where children can burn off excess energy before the flight. Children under 2 years old do not occupy a seat on the plane, and generally, airlines only charge 10% of the adult fare for them.

When booking flights, consider not only the total price and the schedule of your flight but also the cost and time of transfer from the destination airport to Disneyland Paris, as these journeys vary greatly depending on the airport we fly to.

- **Charles de Gaulle Airport (CDG):** It is the largest airport in Paris, located north of the city, 33 km from Disneyland Paris, and it has the simplest and most reasonably priced connections to the park.

- **Orly Airport (ORY):** It is the second most important airport in Paris. It is located south of the capital and 48 km from Disneyland Paris.

- **Beauvais Airport (BVA):** It is a small airport served by low-cost carriers like Ryanair, and is located northwest of Paris, 125 km from the park. Although flight prices are very competitive, being far away makes transfers to the park long and costly.

- **Vatry Airport (XCR)**: It is a small airport far from Paris, 133 km from the park, with practically no flight connections from Spain.

As a general rule, it is advisable to fly to Charles de Gaulle to take the high-speed train (TGV), or to Orly, but we will analyse all the alternatives in the next section.

Transfers: How to Get to the Park from Paris and the Main Airports

Throughout this section, we will see how to get from Paris and the main airports to the train station located right in front of the park entrance, Marne-la-Vallée - Chessy station. This destination stop is unmistakable as it is marked with a Mickey symbol and "Parcs Disneyland". Once there, at the exit, you will find access to Disneyland Park and Walt Disney Studios, as well as Disney Village.

If you're loaded with luggage, you'll need to exit through the side access of the station, where you'll find shuttle bus stops that take you to Disney and partner hotels. Some hotels, such as Hotel New York - The Art of Marvel, are so close that it's worth taking a walk. If you prefer to go directly to the park, in our Luggage Storage and Disney Express section, you'll find tips for storing your luggage and avoiding carrying them on that extra journey.

Transfer from Paris

By RER - A (Suburban Train)

To reach the parks from Paris, you must take the RER-A, "Regional Express Network" (Suburban Train), to Marne-La Vallée Chessy station, at the end of the line. The RER-A (red line) crosses Paris from east to west, with several stops, particularly Châtelet Les Halles and Gare de Lyon in the city center.

The journey takes about 40 minutes, and the price varies depending on the starting station, around €5 per journey for adults, and half price for children aged 4 to 10 (children under 4 travel for free). Ticket vending machines accept credit cards or cash, and you can select the language. It's advisable to buy round-trip tickets for the discount, or at least purchase the return ticket upon arrival at the park station, as there are usually long queues at the vending machines on exit.

Trains run at frequencies between 10 and 25 minutes, and you can check the schedules and stops at www.rera-leblog.fr/horaires

On the Official Disneyland Paris Express Bus

Disneyland Paris offers the option to add transportation from Paris to your one-day tickets on the official bus. The bus departs from 4 stops in central Paris: the Eiffel Tower district, Opéra, Châtelet, and Gare du Nord. You will be accompanied by a bilingual host/hostess fluent in French and English, who will provide you with practical information about the park. Departure times, depending on the station, range from 08:15 to 8:55, and arrival at the park is expected between 9:30 and 9:55, subject to traffic. Time of departure from Disneyland Paris is at 9:00 p.m.

The bus is booked directly on the park's website as part of your ticket package, and the fare depends on the season, starting at around €53 per passenger.

Transfer from CDG, ORY, and BVA Airports

From Charles de Gaulle Airport (CDG)

A) By TGV (High-Speed Train)

The intercity TGV trains are the fastest and most convenient way to reach Disneyland Paris from CDG Airport. It takes about 10 minutes to reach from terminal T2 of the airport to the park train station, Marne-la-Vallée-Chessy.

The ticket price depends on the season, but when purchased in advance, it's around €19 - €20 per one-way trip per adult, about €10 for children between 4 and 11 years old, and free for children under 4. Booking last-minute may vary between a minimum of €15 and a maximum of €37 per person per one-way trip. There are group offers from 10 people. There are two options for reservations and inquiries:

- Through the French SNCF, selecting "Paris - Roissy - Charles de Gaulle" as the origin and "Paris Marne - la Vallée - Chessy" as the destination.

  https://www.sncf-connect.com

- Through "The Train Line" website, which allows adding loyalty cards and sometimes offers additional discounts.

  https://www.thetrainline.com/

A) By Magical Shuttle from CDG

Magical Shuttle is Disney's bus service to reach the park, Disney hotels (excluding Davy Crockett), various partner hotels, and Villages Nature. The service operates 7 days a week. Buses depart from terminal 2F (gate 8) at CDG airport, and from Terminal 1 of the airport, approximately every hour. The journey takes about an hour to the first hotel, and an additional half-hour to the last one, as it stops at all hotels. For the return journey, it is recommended to take the bus from your stop at least 3 and a half hours before the flight check-in at CDG.

The ticket price is €24 for adults, €11 for children under 12, and free for babies up to 2. There is a 10% discount for booking a round trip, and occasionally there are applicable discount codes. Additionally, for groups of 5 to 8 people, a fixed price of €96 per trip can be arranged.

On the service's website, you can make a reservation (which is necessary, especially during peak seasons), check the hotels included in the stops and their exact schedules, and find directions from your terminal to the bus departure point.

https://magicalshuttle.co.uk

As you can see, it's not particularly cheap or fast, but it's comfortable and easy. If you are more than 3 adults, it's worth considering hiring a private transport, which will be equally comfortable and will save you time.

B) By private transport from CDG

For a large group, or during peak pricing periods for the TGV, it's worth considering hiring a private transport service from the airport to the hotel. There are numerous companies offering these services, including Magical Shuttle itself. Vehicles can be equipped with kids car seats upon request. The car journey takes about 40 minutes.

- The Magical Shuttle company itself offers transfers in sedan, van, and even limousine for those with more extravagant budgets! Prices vary depending on the vehicle hired, with economic sedans and vans starting from €117 per trip for 4 people, to €149 for 8 passengers, and can be arranged through their website:

   https://magicalshuttle.co.uk/magical-shuttle-private/

- Other available options include:

   - Paris Shuttle: Their prices are very competitive, ranging from €75 per vehicle. They also provide child seats (€8, upon request). You can book on their website, by phone, or by email.

      https://paris-shuttle.com

   - Private transfers by Civitatis, with prices starting from €91 per vehicle per trip, depending on the season.

      https://www.civitatis.com/en/paris/transfers

C) Other transfer options from CDG to Disneyland Paris:

Although the best speed-price option is usually the TGV, if its price is very high and you are looking to maximise your budget, there are two last options to get from CDG airport to the park:

-   **RER from Charles de Gaulle Airport to Disney**: take the RER B from CDG to Chatelet Les Halles, and once there purchase the RER A ticket, which will take you to Marne la Vallée – Chessy station, near the park. This journey will cost around €20 for adults in total, and 50% for children aged 4 to 11 (free for children under 4), and will take about 1 and a half hours.

-   **Bus 351 + RER A**: The most economical option, but the savings aren't significant considering all the changes and time consumed. Take bus 351 to Nation, and from there, the RER A to Marne la Vallée – Chessy. The total price will be around €15 per person per trip. You can check the bus schedules at www.ratp.fr

From ORLY Airport (ORY)

A) With Magical Shuttle from ORLY

Orly also has the Disney bus service to reach the park and Disney hotels (except Davy Crockett), Villages Nature, and partner hotels. The buses have three stops at the airport, next to terminals 1-2, 3, and 4, respectively. They depart approximately every hour, and the journey takes 1 hour to the first hotel, and an additional half-hour to the last one, as they stop at all hotels. For the return journey, you should take the bus from your stop at least 3 and a half hours before your flight check-in.

The ticket price is €24 for adults, €11 for children under 12, and free for babies between 0 and 2 years old, with a 10% discount for round trips. Occasionally, there are applicable discount codes. Again, it's a comfortable and straightforward option, but not particularly cheap or fast. If there are more than 3 people, it's more cost-effective to hire a private transfer.

On the service's website, you can book your trip (essential during peak season), check the hotels included in the stops and their exact schedules (note that the last one departs from the airport around 7 pm), and how to get from your terminal to each of the three bus departure stops.

https://magicalshuttle.co.uk

B) Private transportation from ORLY to Disneyland Paris

For a large group, the most cost-effective option is to hire a private transfer from Orly Airport to the hotel. Like CDG, there are several companies offering these transportation services, including Magical Shuttle itself, which provides child seats upon request. The car journey takes approximately 55 minutes.

- **Magical Shuttle** offers transfers in sedan, van, or even limousine. The price varies depending on the vehicle hired, starting from €117 per trip for 4 people, up to €149 for 8 passengers.

  https://magicalshuttle.co.uk/magical-shuttle-private/

- Other private transportation options available are:

    - **Paris Shuttle:** They offer very competitive rates, starting from €75 per vehicle. They also provide free child seats (€8, upon request). You can book on their website, by phone, or by email.

      https://paris-shuttle.com

    - **Civitatis Private Transfers,** with an approximate price of €109 per trip per vehicle, depending on the season.

      https://www.civitatis.com/en/paris/transfers

C) Other transportation options from ORLY to Disneyland Paris:

There is one last option to get to Disneyland Paris from Orly Airport, but it is not recommended, as the price is expensive (around €30 per adult) and the journey takes about an hour and a half. However, we mention it so that you have all the available options.

You will have to take the light rail (Orlyval) from Orly Airport to Antony station, and once there, transfer to the RER B, which will take you to Chatelet les Halles in the center of Paris. From this stop, you will need to take the RER A to Marne - La Vallée - Chessy station, the Disneyland Paris station.

From Beauvais Airport (BVA)

Although this airport is quite far from Disneyland Paris, 125 km away from the park, as it is the destination for the low-cost airline Ryanair, it may be your option to maximise your budget, or if it is the best connection from your original airport. It's worth considering, in addition to the flight, the price and time of the transfer to Disneyland Paris.

A) By Aerobus (BusBeauvais) + Metro Line 1 + RER A Train

The most economical option to reach Disneyland Paris from BVA is to take the Aerobus to the metro and then transfer to the suburban train that will take you to the park. Although economical, this option will take you, excluding waiting times, a little over 2 hours from the airport to Disneyland Paris.

Firstly, you should take the Aerobus from the airport to the Porte Maillot metro station. The bus departs at the station located between the two airport terminals, and the schedules are coordinated with the arrivals and departures of Ryanair flights and other airlines operating at Beauvais.

The journey takes 1 hour and 15 minutes and costs €16.90 for adults and €9.90 for children under 12. Additionally, there is a discount for round trips, costing €29.90 and €19.90 respectively.

At Porte Maillot, you should head to Porte Maillot - Neuilly, and from there take Metro Line 1 to Charles de Gaulle - Étoile station. This journey takes 5 minutes and costs about €5, including the train.

Finally, at Charles de Gaulle station, take the RER A train (Suburban) to Marne la Vallée - Chessy - Disneyland Parks station. It takes 45 minutes to reach the destination station, with a frequency of around 10 minutes between trains

You can check the schedules for all three transports on the following websites, although they are subject to change:

Aerobus: http://www.busbeauvais.com

Metro: https://www.ratp.fr/horaires

RER A: https://rera-leblog.fr/horaires/

B) By private transportation from BVA to Disneyland Paris

From Beauvais airport, there is also the option of taking a private shuttle. The car journey lasts approximately 1 hour and 20 minutes, with prices starting from €170 per vehicle per trip. In this case, Paris Shuttle does not operate; other options include Minicab Disney and Civitatis, as well as airport taxis, Uber, etc.

https://www.navettedisney-aeroport.com/en/

https://www.civitatis.com/en/paris/transfers/

Other travel alternatives: by train and by road

A) By train

It is possible to travel by train to Disneyland Paris from the UK. Departing from St. Pancras station in London, the Eurostar will take you to Disneyland Paris in less than 3 hours, with just one transfer. Tickets can be booked on The Train Line, with special rates for young people and children, as well as discounts on your first booking. European countries also offer different train connections with Disneyland Paris.

www.thetrainline.com

B) By road

Taking into account the duration, fuel, and tolls, travelling by car can be worthwhile just in certain cases: if you are more than 4 people, if you live near the French border, or if the trip to Disneyland Paris is part of a larger itinerary through France, visiting the Loire Valley, the Atlantic coast, or any other French destination.

Vehicles can be taken from the UK to France either through the Eurotunnel and through the extensive ferry services towards French ports.

If you're up for it, you can plan the trip with different stops on Via Michelin or Google Maps; keep in mind that you can use the GPS on your phone, as roaming in France is free. Download the map for offline access and monitor consumption if you have limited data.

New charging points for electric vehicles are being installed, both in the Disneyland parking area (in the Infinity parking zone) and in hotels (starting with the newly renovated Disneyland Hotel, Hotel New York - The Art of Marvel and Newport Hotel), and more points are expected to be set up throughout this year. Check with your hotel for availability and configuration of the charging point.

If you're travelling by car, consider staying at the Davy Crockett Ranch or Villages Nature. Both are a bit farther from the park than the rest of the hotels and having your own vehicle is essential to reach them. However, they are surrounded by nature and are a great plan for little explorers.

Whether you stay at a Disney hotel or have an annual pass, parking is free in Disneyland parking lots. The parking fee for other visitors is €30/day. Additionally, most Disney and partner hotels also have plenty of free parking of their own.

If you're planning a road trip, another fun option with kids is travelling in a campervan. Campervans are allowed in the visitor parking lot at Disneyland Paris, although trailer caravans are not permitted. The overnight rate for camper vans is around €45/night (€15 if you have an annual pass), certainly more economical than any hotel, and it will also allow you to experience things in a more independent way, prepare your own meals, save on travel, etc.

In the camper parking area (located next to the bus parking, a little further away than the car parking), there is a shower area (check the opening hours as they are under renovation). It also has a disposal station for wastewater (except in winter, for operational reasons), but there is no electrical connection for camper vans. As it is a parking lot and not a campsite, it is not allowed to set up awnings or camping gear.

If the parking lot is closed (it opens from 8 a.m. to 10 p.m.), there is also an Esso gas station nearby where you can park for free, stock up, fill and empty water for about €5.

Accommodation in Disneyland Paris

There are four types of accommodations near Disneyland Paris, as mentioned earlier:

- Official Disney hotels.
- Partner hotels that have a collaboration agreement with Disney.
- Independent hotels.
- Airbnb accommodations.

As a general rule, the closer they are to the park, the better the hotels... and the higher the prices! From the luxurious Disneyland Hotel (built right above the park's entrance) and the Hotel New York - The Art of Marvel, through the other Disney hotels to the more distant partner hotels and independent hotels, and Airbnb accommodations.

Therefore, the choice will depend on your budget, how many days you plan to visit the park, and the proximity and connections of each accommodation to Disneyland Paris.

Advantages and disadvantages of Disney hotels

There are certain benefits of Disney hotels compared to partner hotels and other accommodations:

1. **Extra Magic Time (EMT) or Extra Magic Hours:** As we mentioned in the "Park Hours" section, guests staying at Disney hotels and Villages Nature, as well as certain annual pass holders, are allowed to access the parks a little earlier than the official opening time. The parks open around 9:30 a.m., and Disney hotel guests can access them from 8:30 a.m., or even a few minutes earlier, and enjoy the parks with fewer crowds. Although not all attractions open during this Extra Magic Time, many do, including some highly sought-after ones like Peter Pan, Big Thunder Mountain, or Buzz Lightyear, as you'll see in our "Lands and Attractions" chart.

However, if you're considering booking a Disney hotel solely for the EMT, but your family struggles to wake up early, and there's a possibility you might arrive late, it's not worth it, as it will cause a lot of stress, which is definitely not the best way to start a vacation day. Instead, with the savings from a more affordable hotel reservation, you can buy Premier Access (One or Ultimate) to enjoy the parks without worries. Disney Premier Access is a paid system to access attractions via the fast lane; you'll find all the details in the "Fast Access to Attractions" chapter.

Another popular option is to spend the previous night at another accommodation, check in early at your Disney hotel, collect the tickets, (or get the Magic Pass online at Disneyland App) and go straight to the park to enjoy the Extra Magic Time.

2. **Distance and connections**: Disney hotels are located within a short distance from the park, no more than 20 minutes on foot. This allows you to avoid buses to the park or partner hotels, which can be slow or crowded. The walk is not unpleasant at all, even from the furthest hotels, as it goes through green areas surrounding the lake. Additionally, all Disney hotels offer a free shuttle bus service to the park, a benefit that some independent hotels or Airbnb accommodations lack. The Davy Crockett Ranch is the exception: it is farther away and does not have a shuttle bus, so it requires having your own vehicle.

3. Theming: Disney Hotels feature special decoration, heavily focused on the Disney world, a gift shop and "Meet and Greet" points with your favourite characters (some of which you can also visit even if you're not staying at those hotels).

Characters typically visit the hotel in the morning and afternoon, so you can take advantage of the EMT to go straight to the park and meet them upon your return. In our "Disney Hotels" section, you'll see which characters visit each one; don't forget to check the schedules at the front desk.

Disney hotels can also help you to start your day on the right foot: nothing better to get the kids going in the morning than receiving a **magical wake-up call.** To schedule it, use the room phone: pick it up, press the clock button or "wake-up", a voice will ask you what time you want to set it for, enter the time (for example, 0730 for 7:30 a.m.), and it will be ready for the next day. Depending on the hotel and the reservation, the character may be Mickey itself or Goofy, and the language could be English, French, or Spanish. However, it could also be Donald, in which case it won't matter much since you can't understand him anyway! You can request your preferred language at the reception desk. Don't forget to set an extra alarm for yourselves so you can record their faces during the call, and you'll have a backup in case it fails.

Additionally, for an extra fee, special room decorations with Disney themes for Halloween, Christmas, birthdays, etc., can be arranged at Disney hotels.

4. Meal Plans: The option to purchase a Breakfast Meal Plan, Half Board, or Full Board is only available to guests staying at Disney hotels. You can find all the information about these packages in our "Meal Plans" section.

5. Restaurant Reservations: Another advantage of Disney hotels is that you can book breakfasts, lunches, and dinners at restaurants with character meet ups, buffets, and table service restaurants in advance, starting from the moment your reservation is paid for. To book the table, simply link your Disney hotel reservation in the app, and the available restaurants will appear at that time.

If you are not staying at a Disney hotel, you can book within 2 months before your stay, although availability may be limited, especially in the most popular ones: Chez Rémy, Captain Jack's, and character dining restaurants like Plaza Gardens and Auberge de Cendrillon.

If you can't manage to book at your preferred restaurant, keep an eye on the app, as they often open available tables (especially around 9 in the morning) if there are cancellations or modifications.

6. Free luggage storage: All Disney hotels, except for Davy Crockett Ranch, offer free luggage storage located near the reception. The luggage storage facilities typically open from 7:30 a.m. to 11:00 p.m., but if you arrive outside of those hours, the reception team can still access them. Additionally, for an extra fee, you can hire **Disney Express Luggage Service**, which provides luggage transfer from Marne-la-Vallée train station to Disney hotels, and vice versa. You'll find all the details in our "Luggage Storage" section.

7. **Shopping transfer service:** All shops in the parks offer Disney Shopping Service, a free service for purchases over €50 made before 3 p.m. With this service, you'll save yourself from carrying the bags all day, and the purchases will be delivered directly to the reception of your Disney hotel (or to Disney Village if you prefer).

8. Free parking is available at both the hotels and the park. If you're not a guest at a Disney hotel, the parking fee for park visitors is €30/day.

9. Deferred payment: The prices for hotel + ticket packages are quite high, but a new feature is the possibility to pay for your reservation in up to 6 instalments.

10. Magic Pass: This card, given to you at reception during check-in, contains all the information about your reservation and facilitates your visit. It serves as your **park ticket**, allowing you to access the park even during Extra Magic Time if you're staying at a Disney hotel.

Additionally, it contains information about any meal plans you've purchased or show seat reservations; it's themed based on the hotel where you're staying and also serves as your room key once available. It also allows you to access the park and hotel parking lots. If you lose it, don't worry, you can request a duplicate at your hotel's reception desk.

Finally, with the card, you'll receive **one hot drink** per person per day at Santa Fe hotel vending machines . Making use of this perk is very simple; you just need to tap the Magic Pass card on the vending machine reader, located in the hotel corridors. Once the green light switches to orange, make your selection (tea, coffee, milk, hot chocolate, etc.), and the machine will dispense your drink. At the rest of Disney hotels, they do not have these machines, as the rooms are equipped with capsule coffee makers and kettles.

During 2024, many of these features (except for room access key and the extra beverage at the vending machines) will be transferred to the new **Digital Magic Pass**, a QR code per person on the reservation, available in the park's app.

This digital Magic Pass is additional: you can have the physical Magic Pass and also have the digital one on your mobile device, which will work with or without an internet connection. With this change, you'll be able to check your meal plan credit in real time (i.e., how many vouchers you've consumed), and even go to the park before stopping by the hotel reception (where, later on, you can pick up the physical Magic Pass to enter the rooms).

11. **Tourist taxes**: Hotel + ticket reservations at Disney hotels booked through the website or a travel agency already include tourist taxes, while in independent accommodations, these taxes are paid separately. This issue is particularly significant this year, due to the Olympic games, as the city has increased all taxes, which, depending on the hotel's star rating and the number of nights you stay, can amount to up to €8 per person per night, starting from approximately €3 for two-star hotels.

However, Disney hotels also have the following **disadvantages** compared to partner hotels and other accommodations:

1. Price: The main drawback of Disney hotels is the high price of the rooms. As you'll see on the official website, the cost per stay is much higher in Disney hotels; not only the room rate but also breakfasts, meals, drinks, etc. We'll include some prices for these extra features in each accommodation review, which will give you a general idea on how it will impact your budget.

2. Comfort and services: Except for the Disneyland Hotel and the Hotel New York - The Art of Marvel, Disney hotels have seen few renovations since their opening, so they appear somewhat outdated compared to similarly rated hotels, specialty when it comes to room comfort and service quality.

3. Breakfast: Disney hotels do not include breakfast, which you'll need to pay for separately or get as part of a Meal Plan. Generally, breakfast at these hotels starts around 7 a.m., to take advantage of Extra Magic Time or in case you have to catch a return flight. In partner hotels, breakfast is included in most cases.

4. Food and equipment: If you want to bring your own food to the park due to allergies or intolerances, to adjust your budget, or simply for personal preference, it's more advisable to book an Airbnb or reserve a bungalow at Villages Nature.

Disney hotels (except for Davy Crockett Ranch) do not have kitchenettes in the rooms, and there's only an individual fridge in the rooms at Disneyland Hotel and New York Hotel - The Art of Marvel.

Disney Hotels

The architecture of each Disney hotel has its own "identity." The Disneyland Hotel, literally located above the park entrance, reflects a Victorian mansion its outside, while the other Disney hotels draw inspiration from different American regions: from the East Coast (Newport Hotel) and New York (Marvel Hotel), to the Wild West (Cheyenne), National Parks (Sequoia Lodge), Route 66 (Santa Fe), and the Canadian border (Davy Crockett Ranch).

Furthermore, each hotel is themed with Disney characters that match the environment in each case, from the Disneyland Hotel, whose palace-inspired interiors are dedicated to "Disney royalty," to the Marvel spirit of the New York Hotel, or the Cars characters of the Santa Fe Hotel.

Hotel Disneyland ★★★★★

The most emblematic, luxurious, and elegant hotel of Disneyland Paris, located right at the entrance of Disneyland Park, reopened its doors in January 2024 after four years of extensive renovation. Inspired by the magic of Disney's most classic fairy tales, it is the quintessential "princess hotel."

The building's architecture has preserved its Victorian inspiration, and the interior decoration gathers details from European castles and palaces, especially from Versailles, combined with thousands of elements from Disney's most "princely" films, from Frozen to Snow White or Sleeping Beauty, as well as Cinderella, Aladdin, The Little Mermaid, Tangled, the Beauty and the Beast..

The different spaces of the hotel have also been completely renovated, unveiling two new restaurants and a bar:

- **"La Table de Lumière"** is the new table service restaurant of the hotel, exclusively accessible for dinner to Disneyland hotel guests. It offers a French-inspired gastronomic proposal and is set in the ballrooms of Versailles and the castle of Beauty and the Beast, with details referencing the film, such as the decoration (each table has its own rose in a glass dome) or exclusive desserts.

  Additionally, during dinner, guests will be accompanied by the "Disney nobility," from Belle herself to Snow White, Ariel, Jasmine and Aladdin, or Sleeping Beauty. Its "Royal Menu" costs 120 € for adults and 60 € for kids ages 3 to 11.

- **"The Royal Banquet":** The new buffet restaurant of the Disneyland hotel is decorated with scenes from the kitchens of Disney classics; from the particular cook of The Little Mermaid to that of Beauty and the Beast, Little John from Robin Hood or Kronk from The Emperor's New Groove. These "chefs" also inspire some of the dishes on this buffet, such as the "Cajun" dishes from Tiana's New Orleans.

  The buffet offers live cooking stations and a selection of international cuisine to satisfy the most discerning palates, including a wide assortment of seafood, products with French Designation of Origin, and Disney desserts. Additionally, during both lunch and dinner, you will receive visits from Disney characters like Mickey and his friends, dressed as princes and princesses.

  The Royal Banquet restaurant has four different rooms, each celebrating a different aspect of the "Disney nobility," from the "Royal Family" room, featuring scenes of Rapunzel's parents, Tiana and her family, or Merida and her brothers, to the "Disney Villains" room.

  Access to the buffet is available for lunch and dinners to guests of all Disney hotels (subject to availability and by adding it to your reservation). Breakfasts will be exclusively available to the Disneyland hotel guests. The prices vary from 45€ for adults breakfast (30€ for kids ages 3 to 11), to 100€ for adults lunch and dinner menus (50 € for child menus).

- **"Fleur de Lys":** The hotel bar is inspired by the Fleur de Lis, the symbol of French nobility, and offers cocktails, snacks, and a selection of wine and champagne in an elegant space overlooking the hotel gardens.

The hotel has completely renovated its 487 rooms, incorporating Disney details and amenities in all of them, which now feature a refrigerator, pillow menu, luxurious amenities, or bathrobes and slippers for children and adults. The rooms are distributed in different categories and price ranges: Superior Rooms, Deluxe, Castle Club, and Suites.

The **346 Superior Rooms** are the first category in terms of price and quality at the Disneyland Hotel. Their silver and blue-toned decoration, adorned with paintings from Disney princess movies, will transport you to the great classics of the Disney factory.

The capacity of the Superior Rooms varies between rooms for 4 people, with 2 double beds, and rooms for 4 people, with one double bed and one fold-down bed. Several of them have a terrace, and there are also family Superior Rooms with a capacity of up to 5 people, equipped with two double beds and one fold-down bed, or two doubles and a sofa bed.

The **82 Deluxe rooms** represent the next category in terms of quality, price, details, and comfort, compared to the Superior rooms. Their decoration, in pink tones, incorporates not only the referred movie paintings and Rapunzel's mirror, but also an illuminated canopy and enchanted artworks that come to life to provide a magical sleeping experience.

The Deluxe rooms have exclusive reception and Lounge areas, where guests can enjoy breakfast in the mornings and snacks in the afternoons, as well as refreshments throughout the day, all included in the room rate.

There are different layouts for the Deluxe rooms: with 2 double beds (accommodating up to 4 people), one double and one fold-down bed (accommodating up to 3 people). There are also Family Deluxe rooms with two double beds and one fold-down bed or two doubles and a sofa bed, accommodating up to 5 people. Additionally, guests can choose between rooms with and without a terrace, with different rates.

The third category is the **Castle Club rooms**, which form a small "hotel within the hotel". They are located on the top two floors and come with a series of exclusive benefits. In addition to a decoration similar to the Deluxe rooms, they have their own reception desk, a private elevator for direct access to Disneyland Park, and access to the Castle Club Lounge.

The **Castle Club Lounge** is an exclusive private salon with views over Disneyland Park and Sleeping Beauty Castle. Its decoration is inspired by Cinderella's art, illustrated by Mary Blair (the creator behind It's a Small World!), and its stained glass windows feature castle decorations that magically light up. In the lounge, guests staying in Castle Club rooms can enjoy buffet and à la carte breakfast accompanied by Disney Princesses in the mornings. In the afternoon you can enjoy some snacks, and soft drinks are served throughout the day, all included in the room rate.

The **Signature Suites** are the most exclusive and spacious rooms in the hotel, ranging from 60 to 90 square metres per suite. There are a total of 16 Signature Suites: 3 for Sleeping Beauty, 3 for Cinderella, 3 for Beauty and the Beast, 3 for Frozen, and 4 for Rapunzel. Reservations for the suites must be made through the park's Disney experts' website.

Each suite is carefully themed and decorated with elements from each movie, not forgetting details with magical lighting effects, such as Rapunzel's golden flower, Cinderella's glass slipper, the rose from Beauty and the Beast, or Sleeping Beauty's dress.

Finally, there are two even more exclusive suites, the "Princely Suite," dedicated to the live-action movie of Beauty and the Beast, and the "Royal Suite," dedicated to Elsa's ice kingdom from Frozen.

The **Princely Suite** features a bedroom and living room, themed with the baroque decoration of the castle, where gold reigns supreme, with a fireplace, chandeliers, and the enchanted rose. Guests will enjoy beautiful views inside Disneyland Park.

The **Royal Suite** is the largest, most exclusive, and luxurious room in Disneyland Paris, transporting guests with its silver and white decoration to Elsa's castle from Frozen. It includes a bedroom, living room, bathroom, kitchen, and dining room, featuring an impressive grand piano, and a balcony with the best views of Disneyland Park, Main Street and Sleeping Beauty Castle.

All 18 suites (including the 16 Signature Suites as well as the Princely and Royal Suites) belong to the Castle Club, so guests enjoy exclusive reception, access to the Castle Club Lounge (including breakfast with princesses, snacks, and refreshments), and a private elevator for direct access to Disneyland Park.

Entertainment at Disneyland Hotel

The **Royal Troupe,** a team of entertainers, roams the hotel, immersing guests in various activities or challenges, such as a magical dust hunt, sometimes with Disney Princesses as protagonists. Additionally, special "ambassadors," the **Story Keepers,** offer guided tours where guests can discover all the secrets and curiosities of the Disneyland Hotel.

The Disneyland hotel features a new "Royal Kids Club" for the little ones, designed as a library where Cast Members welcome children to participate in interactive activities with augmented reality experiences. Additionally, private meetings with Disney princesses such as Snow White, Jasmine, or Ariel can be booked. The hotel also offers a certified babysitting service, free for two hours, for children between 4 and 11 years old.

For children over three years old, the Disneyland hotel offers **"My Royal Dream"** service, a magical experience worthy of the Fairy Godmother. There are three experience packages: Royal Beauty, Royal Makeover, and Royal Makeover Signature, with prices ranging from €95 to €440. All packages include makeup, hairstyling, a photo session, and a framed photo, and the last two also include the costume, which guests can take home after the experience.

The appointment must be booked through the park's app, and although at the time of printing this guide, the service was only available to Disneyland hotel guests, reservations will be opened to more visitors soon. The costume packages are only available in sizes 4 to 14 years old; however, according to park regulations, only children under 12 years old can access with costumes on.

Royal Collection Boutique: The hotel's shop reflects the interior of a palace library, decorated in golden tones with manuscripts and princess emblems. Here you will find park souvenirs and exclusive details from the Disneyland hotel.

Crystal Pool and Health Club: The hotel's pool, inspired by the fabulous greenhouses of Laeken (Belgium), features a modern spa with products and treatments from Clarins (suitable for ages 6 and up), and a gym with state-of-the-art equipment.

The hotel has been designed with the accessibility of all its guests in mind, so all hotel experiences, from the Royal Encounter with characters to the Disneyland Paris Spa or My Royal Dream, are accessible. Additionally, it provides a selection of adapted rooms for guests with reduced mobility, with more space and accessible showers.

To ensure a unique experience for the inaugural guests of the Disneyland Hotel, access to the hotel, reservations for "The Royal Banquet" buffet, and the "My Royal Dream" service were initially limited to hotel guests. Now, reservations for these experiences are gradually being opened to guests from other hotels, and even a certain number of visitors can explore the hotel by booking an access slot through the **Lineberty App**, available for iPhone and Android.

Disney Hotel New York - The Art of Marvel ★★★★

Completely renovated in 2021, this modern 4-star hotel reflects the Marvel universe and the spirit of New York City. It is located less than a 10-minute walk from the park entrance and just steps away from the free shuttle bus service to the park and Disney Village. Decorating its walls, serving as an "art gallery", are hundreds of works featuring Marvel superheroes, with each floor dedicated to one of them, from Thor to Iron Man, Hulk, or Spider-Man.

The hotel offers 565 rooms and suites with different categories and prices, depending on whether they have lake views and their capacity (from 3 to 6 people). Requests for connecting rooms or adjacent non-connecting rooms should be made at the time of booking. Additionally, there are certain VIP rooms, as part of the Empire State Club, which come with extra amenities and a private lounge bar, as well as a Presidential Suite with multiple floors and a grand piano, for those who deem it "essential".

Rooms are equipped with air conditioning, Wi-Fi, capsule coffee maker, amenities, fridge... Upon request, guests can have a crib and kettle added to their room. Additionally, guests have access to 24-hour room service, free luggage storage, valet parking, and a concierge service.

In addition, you can make use of the following spaces:

- The **Downtown Athletic Club,** open from 8 a.m. to 10 p.m., offers a spa, massages (for a fee), gym, outdoor tennis courts, running track, and indoor and outdoor heated pool. Additionally, in the outdoor training area "Hero Training Zone," you can practice basketball, fitness, and yoga.

- **Super Hero Station:** Like in all Disney hotels, there are scheduled character visits, and the New York Hotel features Marvel superheroes at this meeting point. The superheroes may vary depending on the release of their movies or series, although the most common ones are Spider-Man and Black Widow; and you must reserve the encounters through the App.

  Check with reception for morning and evening schedules to try to coincide with them. This spot is only accessible to hotel guests, unlike other Disney hotels where you can approach their Meet Points.

- **Marvel Design Studio**: Following the theme of the "Marvel Art Gallery" of the hotel, this design room is for children aged 3 to 12, who must be accompanied by an adult. Here, kids can become Marvel artists as the studio is equipped with drawing stations, toys, colouring sheets, interactive games, etc.

- **Manhattan Restaurant:** A sophisticated Italian-style table-service restaurant where you can enjoy pasta, lasagne, risottos, etc. Menu prices start from €45/adult and €25/child. It's advisable to check with reception for the opening hours as it may be closed, and booking in advance is recommended, as restaurants at the New York Hotel tend to be quite busy.

- **Downtown Restaurant:** A New York-style buffet restaurant where you can have breakfast or dinner. The price for breakfast is €28/adult and €23/child. The dinner buffet, priced at €45/adult and €25/child, offers an international selection with American, Italian, Asian dishes, and of course, plenty of Avengers-themed desserts. The quality is superior to other options in the park, making it very popular, so reservations are recommended.

- **Skyline Bar:** Beers and cocktails in a modern New York-style bar.

- **New York Boutique:** The hotel's shop, focused on the Marvel universe: toys, merchandise, prints, and even hotel bathrobes and slippers to remember the experience.

- **Bleecker Street Lounge:** Beers, soft drinks, and sweet and savoury snacks in this comfortable New York loft-style bar.

This hotel is a well located and comfortable option, but it's also on the pricier side. If your budget allows, it's the best choice if your kids are big fans of superheroes. It's also a great option if you want to enjoy higher-quality meals, as the restaurants at the New York Hotel are among the best within the park and hotels. Furthermore, if your children are budding artists or huge Marvel comics fans, there's a tour of the hotel to see all the artworks.

Disney Newport Bay Club ★★★★

Located at the lake shore, this coastal-themed hotel is inspired by New England's maritime clubs and resorts. The decoration, in white, blue, and wood tones, is purely nautical, with Captain Mickey details. It is located 1 km (a 15-minute walk) from the park entrance, or a 5-minute shuttle bus ride away.

It is the largest hotel in the park, with nearly 1,100 rooms and 13 suites (in fact, when it opened, it was the largest hotel in Europe), some of which, at a higher price, have views of the lake and its iconic lighthouse. The other options face the rear, which is a bit more crowded and less serene.

Standard room capacity is up to 4 people, plus one child under 3 years old, and there are family rooms available for 6 people (they are limited, so booking well in advance is highly recommended). Rooms are equipped with a TV and hairdryer, and some include a coffee maker, but not a fridge (there is only a coffee and ice machine in the hallway).

The main building (Admiral Floor), which houses the reception and concierge, the bar, the two restaurants, and the VIP area on the first floor, leads to two large wings, one to the East and one to the West, and a convention center.

In the East wing, you'll find the pool, the gym, and some of the rooms, while the West wing houses the rest of the rooms. The hotel also features a VIP area, the Compass Club, on the top floor, with luxurious rooms, private reception, and lounge, and some "Honeymoon" suites in the lighthouse area.

Check-in can be done at any time of the day, and rooms will be available from 3 p.m. You can leave your luggage at the luggage storage, head to the park, and pick them up upon your return. The luggage storage is located just before the main entrance, on the opposite side of the lake, and if it's closed upon your return, you'll have access to your luggage at the reception.

The hotel offers the following spaces and restaurants:

- **Cape Cod Buffet:** A buffet restaurant where you can enjoy breakfast or dinner. The price for breakfast is around €38 for adults and €23 for children, and dinner costs €45 for adults and €25 for children, including drinks. The cuisine is international, with a focus on seafood, and desserts often feature Mickey and Minnie-themed decorations.

- **Yacht Club:** A table-service restaurant with views of the lake and lighthouse, specialising in seafood. The decor is entirely nautical, and menu prices start from €55 for adults and €30 for children, although à la carte options are also available, as in all Disney table-service restaurants. Reservations are necessary.

- **Captain's Quarters Bar:** Coffee, soft drinks (€6!), snacks, and cocktails (approximately €15) are served in this bar reminiscent of ship cabins. Please check opening hours.

- **Little Captain's Corner:** A play area where children can paint, and a video game room, the "Sea Horse Club Game Room".

- **Bay Boutique:** A small shop offering a selection of Disney merchandise.

- **Meet and Greet:** The characters at these encounters have a nautical theme, such as Mickey, Minnie, or Goofy in their sailor outfits, Captain Hook, or Mr. Smee from Peter Pan.

- **Nantucket Pool:** The indoor pool is smaller than in other hotels, partly occupied by a huge boat; but it also has a very pleasant outdoor area. Towel service and lockers are available, and it generally opens from 7 am to 10 pm; you can inquire about specific hours at the reception.

- **Parking** is free, with a small charging area for electric vehicles, and a paid valet parking service.

In a hotel of this size, the hallways can be quite long, and it takes as much time to go back and forth to the room as it does to the park itself! When checking in, the closer your room is to the main building and the East wing, the better, to save on travel time. Guests staying in rooms further away sometimes bring a toiletry kit with a toothbrush to breakfast, so they don't have to return to the room before heading to the park!

In summary, although it's a beautiful hotel in terms of location, architecture, pool, etc; the rooms urgently need an update to meet the expectations of a 4-star hotel. This includes adding a refrigerator to the rooms, bedside sockets, and improving amenities. It's pleasant in winter (all spaces are connected by covered corridors, and its shorter distance to the park will make your travels easier) and also in summer, due to its cool surroundings by the lake.

Disney Hotel Cheyenne ★★★

This Western-themed hotel consists of different buildings around a central street, immersing you in a cowboy movie setting. Woody, Jesse, and the horse Bullseye from Toy Story are the "hosts" of this Wild West experience. It's located about a 20-minute walk from the park entrance, passing through the Hotel New York and the Village, or a 5-minute ride on the free shuttle bus, which runs every 10 minutes.

It offers over 1,000 rooms, with prices varying depending on whether they have river views or not, and their location within the complex. Rooms accommodate up to 4 people, and adjoining rooms can be requested at the time of booking. All rooms feature air conditioning, a fan, Wi-Fi, TV, telephone, bathtub, hairdryer, and upon request, a crib or kettle can be provided.

As for services and facilities, you can enjoy the following:

- **Reception** (available 24 hours), along with a laundry service (for a fee), luggage storage, and concierge service, as well as free parking.

- **Chuck Wagon Café:** A buffet-style restaurant for breakfast and dinner, decorated in a rodeo style. Some ingredients are sourced from the hotel's own orchard, offering local food! Reservations are essential. The dinner buffet (specialising in barbecue and ribs) costs €40/adult and €22/child, including drinks; breakfast is approximately €20/adult and €15/child.

- **Red Garter Saloon:** Soft drinks (€5), cocktails (€15), and sweet and savoury snacks are served in this bar decorated as an authentic American saloon.

- **Starbucks:** A branch of this classic coffee chain, where you can grab a quick coffee or snack on the way to the park.

- **General Store**: The hotel's shop resembles a Wild West warehouse, offering a selection of cowboy-themed souvenirs, snacks, and Disney toys.

In terms of leisure activities at the hotel, despite not having a pool, it's a fun option for children due to its well-executed theme and indoor playroom and outdoor children's areas, such as tepees, wagons, and a fort.

It's a great choice in summer because the rooms have air conditioning and ceiling fans, and the hotel also takes advantage of the good weather to organise pony rides for the little ones, for an additional fee. In winter, you can gather around the outdoor campfire, next to the Red Garter Saloon.

Disney Sequoia Lodge ★★★

Located within a 10-15 minute walk from the park entrance, which can also be reached by free shuttle bus, this hotel is inspired by the movie Bambi and the American national parks such as Yosemite, Yellowstone, or Big Sur. As expected, during character encounters, Mickey, Minnie, or Chip and Dale will appear dressed in "park ranger" style clothing.

When booking your room, you can choose between rooms with and without lake views, both standard categories and suites. The hotel has over 1,000 standard rooms and 15 suites, spread across a main building with two wings where the reception, restaurants, and most of the rooms are located, and 6 secondary buildings named after each national park, where the pool, fitness center, and the rest of the rooms are situated.

Although the hotel does not have family rooms, and the maximum capacity is 4 adults and 1 baby on a crib, you can request adjacent and connected rooms. Additionally, it features a "VIP" section, the Golden Forest Club, with more luxurious rooms, private reception and lounge.

Furthermore, the Sequoia Lodge hotel offers the following services and restaurants:

- **Redwood Bar and Lounge:** The hotel's bar where you can enjoy hot drinks, beer, or cocktails (€6-15), along with sandwiches or sweets (€5-15), around the fireplace.

- **Hunter's Grill Restaurant:** A rustic-style buffet restaurant where you can have breakfast (reservations recommended) or dinner featuring meats, fish, etc. The price for the dinner buffet is €45 for adults and €25 for children, including drinks. For the same price, there are more themed or better-stocked restaurants in the Village.

- **Beaver Creek Tavern:** (currently under renovation)

- **Little Prairie:** A children's area with cartoons and video games where kids can be entertained (always accompanied by their parents).

- **Northwest Passage Shop**: This shop offers a wide range of Disney merchandise, toys, souvenirs, etc., as well as park "must-haves" like Mickey ears or water bottles. The storefront is very appealing, with figures of Mickey and Donald's nephews on an adventure through the sequoia forest.

It's a good option, relaxing and peaceful, all year round: in autumn and winter it's perfect, with its warm and cosy fireplace lounge and pleasant heated pool (with an outdoor area, and slides that will delight children). In spring and summer, it's also a great choice, as the surroundings are very enjoyable, with lots of trees, including giant sequoias brought from the United States.

Disney Hotel Santa Fe ★★

This hotel, built around a "volcano", is themed after Route 66 and the southern border of the United States. It was renovated in 2013, completing it with the characters from "Cars". It's located about a 20-minute walk from the park entrance, which can be reached by walking along the river and the Marvel New York Hotel. It also has a free shuttle service, which runs every 10 minutes and takes about 8 minutes to reach the park; and, again, like in all Disney hotels, you can access the parks during Extra Magic Time.

It offers approximately 1,000 rooms, distributed in 4 areas, named after Lightning McQueen, Sally, Mater, and Luigi. Room prices vary in three ranges: depending on whether they are located near the central building (where the reception or restaurant is located); near the river (closer to the path to the park), or farther away from both.

The standard capacity of the rooms is 4 people plus one child under 3 years old (with cribs and bed rails available upon request). They also have a limited number of family rooms for 6 people.

The hotel offers free Wi-Fi and luggage storage, concierge service, and a safe-deposit box at the reception, as well as the following spaces:

- **La Cantina:** A buffet restaurant where you can have breakfast or dinner, set in a car repair shop theme, serving American-style food. The breakfast price is €21 for adults and €14 for children, while dinner costs €35 for adults and €22 for children. Reservations are necessary.

- **Starbucks Café:** A café from this classic chain where you can have coffee or a snack on your way to the park.

- **Trading Post:** The hotel's store selling souvenirs, ear hats, clothing, toys, and a small selection of snacks and drinks, featuring Lightning McQueen and his friends from Radiator Springs.

- **Character Meet-and-greets:** Check with reception for the schedule both in the morning and evening at the hotel lobby. Typically, Mickey, Goofy, and Minnie are dressed in Mexican-themed attire in line with the hotel's decor.

Additionally, in front of the hotel, there is an Esso gas station with a small shop, in case you want to pick up snacks, drinks, or bread to take to the park, or even if you need a mobile charger, cap, or sunglasses...

Hotel Santa Fe is the most budget-friendly accommodation option at a Disney hotel if you don't have your own vehicle. It's not the most recommended option in summer, as it doesn't have air conditioning or shaded areas, and the rooms are exposed to the sun for most of the day.

Davy Crockett Ranch ★★★

The last of the Disney hotels is not a typical hotel but rather a collection of wooden cabins or bungalows surrounded by a forest, from where you can reach the park in a 15-minute drive. The resort does not offer a shuttle service, so you will need your own vehicle if you want to stay there. Although very basic in terms of services and amenities, if you're travelling by car, it's the most economical option among the Disney hotels and ideal in many cases: if you're nature lovers or if you need to disconnect from the hustle and bustle of the park from time to time. Additionally, Disneyland Paris has announced that its bungalows will undergo a renovation during 2024, to provide a modern and more comfortable experience for guests.

Children will love experiencing something different in this "camp" style reminiscent of "boy scouts" Additionally, like all Disney accommodations, you'll enjoy Extra Magic Time to access the parks before opening hours.

It's the only Disney hotel that doesn't have luggage storage, so you'll need to leave your luggage in the car (or take it to the park and store it there) until you check-in into your cabin. You can park in front of each cabin or at the guest parking at the park, at no additional cost.

The ranch offers two types of cabins, Standard and Premium, with capacity, except for exceptions, for 6 people. All of them have Wi-Fi, and although they are close to each other, they are generally quiet since visitors are usually at the park most of the day, and the cabins are surrounded by vegetation.

- **Standard Cabins:** These bungalows accommodate up to 6 people and feature a bathroom, bed linens and towels, air conditioning, TV, and a small but equipped kitchen with microwave, refrigerator, dishwasher, coffee maker, kitchenware etc. Outside each cabin, there's a small terrace with a barbecue, a picnic table, and a parking space for your vehicle. The cleaning kit, including dishwasher detergent and others, is available at reception.

- **Premium Cabins:** Premium bungalows feature all the amenities of the standard cabins and some extras, such as additional privacy, thanks to its private patio, and extra comfort, with a better equipped kitchen, with coffee and tea makers. Other upgrades include bathroom amenities, a hairdryer, slippers, and a bathrobe. The cleaning kit is already provided.

The Davy Crockett Ranch also offers the following spaces and services:

- **Crockett's Tavern:** A buffet-style restaurant serving Tex-Mex cuisine, available for dinner (reservations required). The dessert selection is particularly varied, including some themed options. The menu, including drinks, costs €35 for adults and €22 for children.

- **Breakfast:** There isn't a lobby or cafe at the hotel where you can have breakfast; instead, it's a Take Away service that you'll need to collect with your Magic Pass. The reception will inform you of your collection point, which you can reach by car or on foot. It might seem like a hassle, but if the weather is nice, it's a pleasant 5-minute walk surrounded by trees, very peaceful and quiet, listening to the birds and, if you're lucky, spotting some squirrels, badgers, or hedgehogs. The breakfast box includes a choice of coffee or tea, milk or juice, some bread, pastries, etc.

  Without a meal plan, breakfast costs €12 per person. The breakfast collection cabins open at 7:30 a.m., so considering the distance to the park, it's advisable to take it with you if you want to make the most of the Extra Magic Time.

- **Alamo Trading Post:** In addition to the usual souvenirs and toys from the park, this store offers a selection of "essentials" to make your stay at the ranch more comfortable; from mineral water to basic ingredients, or toiletries. To summarise, it's more or less like a Carrefour Mini selection, but at slightly higher prices.

One of the best plans at the ranch is to have a small homemade barbecue on the cabin's terrace. At Alamo Trading Post, you'll find everything you need (such as charcoal, firelighters, bread, meat, fish, and vegetables...). The only thing missing is coffee machine filters, so keep that in mind if you can't survive without caffeine!

- For the more adventurous, there's the Davy Crockett Adventure, an exploration trail with swings, trapezes, rope bridges, and stairs. There are some tennis courts, video games arcades and pony rides, activities that may include an extra fee. Additionally, the ranch has perhaps the most fun pool of all the Disney hotels, with a waterfall, "river" pool, slide, and, for your convenience, towel service.

- If you're travelling with dogs, Davy Crockett Ranch is the only Disney Hotel that allows pets in certain rooms (at a cost of €30/day, which doesn't include food but does include an accessories kit). The dog must be properly identified with a microchip and vaccinated (a vaccination certificate is required), and cannot belong to the dangerous breeds according to French regulations. You can check the conditions and reserve these services on the website and through the Customer Service phone line.

Partner Hotels

The partner hotels or associated hotels are a series of accommodations that have a collaboration agreement with Disney. This means that Disney recommends them for their quality and location, and they can be booked directly from the park's website. All of these options have a direct shuttle bus to the park.

- Hôtel l'Elysée Val d'Europe ★★★★
- Campanile Val de France ★★★
- Explorers Fabulous Hotels Group ★★★
- B&B Hôtel ★★
- Staycity Aparthotels Paris, Marne . La Vallée ★★★★
- Adagio Serris / Marne-La Vallée Val d'Europe – Apartments ★★★

Hôtel l'Elysée Val d'Europe ★★★★

7 Cr du Danube, 77700 Serris. Tel. +33 1 64 63 33 33

The partner hotel L'Elysée Val D'Europe, with a Parisian style, is located just minutes away from the Val D'Europe shopping center and the Sea Life aquarium. It's also 2 km from Disneyland Paris, which can be reached by a free shuttle bus. Additionally, it offers luggage storage, private parking, and the RER Val D'Europe train station connects to the park in 2 minutes and to Paris in 35 minutes.

Its over 150 rooms, including standard, family, and adapted rooms, feature air conditioning and free Wi-Fi, and you can request a crib in your reservation.

The restaurant, with a lovely terrace, serves French and international cuisine, as well as a breakfast buffet and a children's menu. Moreover, through a small garden with a walkway, you can access the bar from the restaurant, where you can enjoy a cocktail.

The hotel is modern, well-equipped, and tastefully decorated; however, it might not be the best choice for families with children, as the majority of guests are couples seeking tranquillity in a charming hotel. Despite this, it does offer a children's area and entertainment.

Hotel Campanile Val de France ★★★

10 Av. de la Fosse des Pressoirs, 77700 Magny-le-Hongre. www.campanile.com

The Hotel Campanile Val de France is an economical and comfortable accommodation, suitable for the entire trip or for overnight stays before or after your visit to a Disney hotel. It's located about 10 minutes from the park via a free shuttle bus. It offers 300 rooms, accommodating from 4 to 6 people, equipped with air conditioning, free Wi-Fi, TV, bathtub, and hairdryer.

Its restaurant "Le Marché Gourmand" offers buffet dinners and breakfasts (not included) from 8:30 to 11 a.m. Additionally, the L'Abrevoir bar serves snacks and nibbles throughout the day, and the hotel also has a Sushi Bar and a Burger Bar open from 6 to 11 p.m.

The establishment features a 24-hour reception and free luggage storage (located in a separate building), as well as a Disney store (with shopping shuttle service from the park, as an exception). It's a child-friendly hotel, with a carousel, video game room, and a covered children's area, along with a pleasant environment with a lake and a small farm (its ponies, goats, and rabbits will delight the little ones).

Explorers Fabulous Hotels Group ★★★

50 Av. de la Fosse des Pressoirs, 77700 Magny-le-Hongre. www.explorershotels.com

Perhaps the most "family-friendly" among the partner hotels, this accommodation is specifically designed for families with children. It's located about 20 minutes from the park via a free shuttle bus. It offers nearly 400 rooms, including family rooms and contiguous rooms accommodating up to 10 guests, with baby cots available upon request. The rooms, except for the suites, do not have air conditioning, just ceiling fans.

One of the appeals of this hotel is that it includes free access to the visitor parking lot at Disneyland, in addition to its own parking lot, making it a good option if you're travelling with your own vehicle. Additionally, it features a reception desk (open 24 hours), free luggage storage, and Wi-Fi. The breakfast buffet is included, and the hotel has several restaurants, a pizzeria, a bar, a snack kiosk, and even a candy store. Moreover, you can find a small convenience store for unexpected needs.

The hotel is inspired by the world of pirates and mermaids, with indoor and outdoor children's play areas, a ball pit, a video game room, a kids' fitness centre, and even a cinema. The indoor pool is very entertaining, featuring a large pirate ship, slides (requiring tight-fitting swimwear), and a surprise waterfall.

B&B Hôtel ★★

60 Av. de la Fosse des Pressoirs, 77700 Magny-le-Hongre. www.hotel-bb.com

The B&B Hotel at Disneyland Paris is located next to the Explorers Hotel, 3 km from the Disneyland Paris parks, which can be reached within 10 minutes using the free shuttle service. It's a simple and economical hotel, a bit basic in terms of updates and amenities, but it provides the essentials for spending the day at the park and returning just to sleep. Parking is free if you're travelling with your own vehicle.

The 400 rooms, accommodating up to 5 people and with cots available upon request, feature air conditioning and free Wi-Fi. The hotel has a multipurpose room with an ATM, a play area, vending machines, and a microwave for children's food. You can opt for the buffet breakfast or grab something to eat at the "Les Halles" restaurant and the bar.

The reception is open 24 hours, and they offer luggage storage service (with an extra cost of 2 €, payable in cash) to store your luggage until your room is available (from 3:00 p.m.), or after check-out at 11:00 a.m. One thing to bear in mind is that the tourist tax, approximately €5 per person per night, is not included.

Villages Nature Paris at Disneyland® Paris ★★★★

Rte de Villeneuve, 77700 Bailly-Romainvilliers. Tel. +33 1 61 10 77 77

About 6 km from the park, you'll find this new concept of premium accommodation, offering nearly 900 apartments and cabins. This accommodation comes with certain Disney-associated benefits and can be booked directly from the Disneyland website along with park tickets. Its Magic Pass card allows access to the park during Extra Magic Time.

A unique aspect of this hotel is that bookings through the Disneyland Paris website include only two days of park tickets, unlike other Disney and partner hotels, which include as many tickets as nights booked, plus an extra day. For example, booking for 4 nights at Villages Nature will provide tickets for two consecutive days of park access. This is due to the wide range of entertainment options available at the hotel: it's the perfect choice for those looking to enjoy experiences beyond Disneyland. It features a large lake suitable for swimming, a water park with pools, a farm, gardens, a children's play forest, a bowling alley, and a host of activities that kids will love.

In terms of price, concept, and location, it's similar to the Davy Crockett Ranch, but more modern and with better services and facilities, including a restaurant area around the lake, a small supermarket, and a bakery. Breakfast is not included, and its price starts at €14. There are several room categories available, accommodating up to 6 people, equipped with a kitchen, wifi, hairdryer, bathtub, etc.

Regarding transfers to the park, it's about a 15-minute drive by own vehicle (with free parking available) or a 25-minute shuttle bus ride (for a fee). A small downside of this accommodation is that the check-out is before 10 a.m., and like the Davy Crockett Ranch, it doesn't offer luggage storage.

Staycity Aparthotels Paris, Marne . La Vallée ★★★★

All. de l'Orme Rond, 77700 Bailly-Romainvilliers. Tel. +33 1 72 18 03 60

The newest addition to the partner accommodations of Disneyland Paris, available on their website, is this aparthotel located 10 minutes away from the Disney Park by free shuttle bus. It features apartments with capacity for 4 to 5 people, equipped with a full kitchen, espresso machine, bathtub, wifi, and other amenities. The aparthotel offers a restaurant with breakfast buffet and a bar, the Staycafé. Additionally, guests can enjoy its heated indoor pool with a lovely outdoor area, a gym, a children's play area (under parental supervision), and a recreation area (at an additional cost).

Adagio Marne-La-Vallée Val d'Europe - Apartments

42 Cours du Danube, Serris. www.adagio-city.com

This aparthotel is located about 3km from the park, approximately a 10-minute shuttle bus ride or 20-minute walk. The apartments are spacious, equipped with a kitchen, and can accommodate up to 7 people, although they are in need of renovation.

It is a good value-for-money option if you are a large group, planning to stay for several days (thus not needing to be very close to the park), or prefer not to have many meals in the park, as they come with a kitchen and are located next to a shopping centre with a supermarket. There is also the option to have a buffet breakfast in their lounge.

It offers a children's corner in the lobby and an indoor heated pool open all year round (except for specific dates in June and January). The reception is open 24 hours, there is free Wi-Fi connection, and covered parking.

There is another option of Adagio apartments not associated with Disney, even closer to the park: the Adagio Serris Val d'Europe, which we will review below.

Independent hotels

In the vicinity of the Disney Park, in the towns of Serris and Chessy, there are several non-associated hotels that you can consider if you purchase your tickets independently. However, not all of them provide easy access by train or bus to the park and the station.

While there are countless options, we will outline the two most relevant ones due to their previous relationship with Disneyland Paris: the Adagio Serris Val d'Europe apartments and the Grand Magic Hotel.

Adagio Serris Val d'Europe Apartments ★★★

18, Cours de l'Elbe, 77700 Serris. www.adagio-city.com

Apartments are located next to the shopping center and the Val d'Europe station, a 10-minute shuttle bus ride from the park (or a 2-minute journey by RER train). You can also walk to the park in about 20 minutes. It is an aparthotel with independent studios and suites, modern and equipped with a kitchen, from the same chain as the associated Adagio Marne - la Vallée aparthotel. It offers free Wi-Fi, air conditioning, an outdoor pool (open from May to September), a gym, and a massage center. Breakfast buffet can be arranged, and baby cots can be added (subject to availability).

Grand Magic Hotel ★★★★

20 Av. de la Fosse des Pressoirs, Magny-le-Hongre. www.grand-magic-hotel.com

Formerly known as Magic Circus, it has been transformed into an independent hotel, meaning it is no longer associated with Disney, but it remains a good option for mid to high budgets, especially if you have purchased tickets separately with a discount. Inspired by French countryside mansions, it is located about 10 minutes from the park by free shuttle bus. The shuttle bus is taken at the "Bus stop Q", it runs every 20 minutes, and connects the hotel with the Marne-la-Vallée station and the park entrance.

It offers nearly 400 rooms and suites, ranging from double rooms to connected family rooms, accommodating up to 8 people, with different price ranges.

The hotel features a bar and two restaurants where you can enjoy the buffet breakfast (complimentary, included in the price) or a table service dinner. It was renovated in 2022. Additionally, its facilities include an indoor pool, fitness room, and game room, and it is surrounded by beautiful gardens with a terrace and children's play area.

Parking is free, with capacity for 300 vehicles. You can book a transfer from the airport through the hotel, or, as mentioned, take the shuttle bus from the Marne-La Vallée train station. Shuttle bus schedules can be found at:

https://www.navette-hotels-valdefrance.com/en/accueil

AirBnb and Homeaway

You'll find a multitude of apartments available in the Val d'Europe and Serris area, about 5 km from Disneyland Paris. To reach the parks, you can take the commuter train from the Val d'Europe station, which will take you to the Marne-la-Vallée-Chessy station in less than 5 minutes, or take a 20-minute walk.

In general, they are a very economical option, not only because of the accommodation price but also because you can prepare breakfasts and meals, thus adjusting your budget. For this, you have a large supermarket in the Val d'Europe shopping center where you can buy everything you need.

Meal Plans

Meal plans are **dining packages** with different options that you can add to your Disneyland hotel reservation (they cannot be purchased if you stay at a partner hotel or an independent one). You can add them either at the time of booking or later, up to a week before your trip, but don't forget these plans have to be booked before your stay. In our "Restaurants" chapter, you'll find reviews, estimated prices, and ambiance of each restaurant so you can assess the complete offer.

You can also modify or even cancel meal plans before your trip, for example, if you can't get a reservation at any of the restaurants you're interested in. Another option is to book the restaurants first and then add the meal plan to your hotel reservation once your table has been confirmed.

Meal plans are purchased for **all members** included on the hotel reservation and for **every day of the stay**. This means that if you opt for a meal plan, it must be for all members of the group, except children under 3 years old. For children aged 3 to 11, there is a reduced price for the child rate. Also, it's not possible to, for example, purchase a Breakfast Plan for individual days; the meal plan you choose applies to all days of the reservation.

Meal Plan Options

There are three meal plans available: Breakfast (at a Disney hotel), Half Board (breakfast + 1 meal/dinner daily), or Full Board (breakfast + 2 meals daily + 1 meal on the last day).

Furthermore, within the meal plans, there are **different options** for all budgets:

- **Standard:** This option provides access to 35 restaurants, including table service, buffet, and quick-service restaurants. At least one of the daily meals on the Full Board plan must be taken at a quick-service restaurant. You can find the list of included restaurants on the website, which includes all park restaurants (except for the two character dining restaurants, Auberge de Cendrillon and Plaza Gardens, where you would pay the price difference), as well as several restaurants in the hotels and Disney Village. Prices start from €30 for children and €50 for adults on the Half Board plan.

- **Plus:** With this option, you have access to the same 35 restaurants, but it's not mandatory for any of the daily meals to be at a quick-service restaurant. Prices start from €40 per child and €60 per adult.

- **Premium:** This option is only available for Disneyland hotel guests and adds four extra options to the 35 restaurants available for the Plus and Standard plans, including the Disneyland hotel restaurants, The Royal Banquet, and La Table de Lumière. Prices for this option start from €70 for children and €125 for adults on the Half Board plan.

- **Extra Plus:** Although currently unavailable, this option is perfect for those with more generous budgets. The Extra Plus Meal Plan, in addition to the conditions of the Plus Plan, includes an extra beverage and snack, and one of the meals or dinners (excluding breakfast) can be at a character dining restaurant (choose between lunch or dinner at Auberge de Cendrillon or dinner at Plaza Gardens, as characters do not visit during lunch). You can find reviews of both in our Restaurants chapter.

In your Magic Pass (physical or digital), you will find your meal vouchers loaded. If you have the Half Board Meal Plan, you can use one voucher for lunch and another voucher for dinner on the same day; it is not limited to only one voucher per day. Whatever Meal Plan option you choose, lunch and dinner vouchers are accepted for their monetary value in all restaurants in the Disney Parks and Disney Hotels as well as in some of the restaurants at Disney Village. Breakfast vouchers are also accepted for their monetary value in a selection of restaurants in the Disney Parks and Disney Village.

As previously mentioned, if the restaurant you visit is not included in your plan, or if you want a menu option that is not included, the value of the voucher will be deducted from the bill, and you will only pay the difference. In any case where the total fee exceeds the value of the meal, you will have to pay the difference. No refund will be issued if the total is lower than the value of the meal included in your plan. Please note that starting from March 2024, beverages in table service restaurants for adults and desserts in quick-service restaurants will no longer be included in the Meal Plan.

Is it worth getting the Meal Plans?

Is it worth it? The answer is… it depends!

- Firstly, Disney periodically offers meal plan deals that are worth taking advantage of, especially for breakfasts, which are not included in the room rate. Additionally, you can add them to your reservation not only when purchasing tickets/accommodation but also up to a week before your arrival.

- At full price, without special deals, it's difficult for the Meal Plan to be cost-effective, unless you choose to 'make the most of it' at all times".

When do you make the most of a Meal Plan?

When you always have breakfast at the hotel buffet, and dine at table-service restaurants, character dining or buffet restaurants (included in your plan or paying the extra for each one). In other words, if you plan to choose the fancier options.

When is the Meal Plan not worth it?

The truth is that, when travelling with small children or with little time, it's difficult for the Meal Plan to be worthwhile. Let's see several examples:

-   If you're short on time: table service restaurants tend to have slower service, and you can lose a lot of time at each meal. Quick service restaurants, especially when ordering in advance with Mobile Food Order, are much faster, allowing you to get back to enjoying attractions quickly.

-   It also may not be worth it if you want to take full advantage of the Extra Magic Time by being in the park before anyone else, simply grabbing drinks from the machine and a quick breakfast on the go. Or if you choose to have something at the Village (where some restaurants are not included in the Meal Plan), either at park closing, as they tend to stay open later, or before catching your return flight, as they are usually less crowded.

-   It also may not be worthwhile if your children, like many, choose something very simple from the menu or eat very little (take a look at the park menus before purchasing the plans; the park's food might not suit you, and the food at the Village restaurants not included in the plans might).

-   On the other hand, meal plans also may not be worth it if any family member has a specific diet and needs to bring their own food to the park (check our section on Allergies and Celiac Disease for more advice on this), as the plans have to be purchased for the entire reservation. Another option is to make two separate reservations, but this often leads to more logistical issues.

-   Lastly, if you're on a tighter budget, and opt, for example, to bring snacks, have a quick lunch at fast-food restaurants or kiosks in the park, and a heartier 'snack-dinner' at the McDonald's in the Village. Both parks allow you to bring in food or drinks, but only in reasonable amounts: sandwiches and snacks, except in the case of allergies, celiac disease, and baby food. You can also use the picnic area near the visitor parking lot.

Fast access to attractions

Disney Premier Access

Disney Premier Access is a paid system to skip lines and access 15 of the attractions in the two parks through the fast queue. It replaces the old free Fastpasses and the Genie+ system in the American parks, and it has two options: Disney Premier Access One and Disney Premier Access Ultimate.

- **Disney Premier Access One:** It's a fast access pass that you can purchase through the app on the same day, once you enter the park, for the attraction you're interested in. With your reservation linked to your account, you can choose which attraction and for whom.

  The App will show you schedules and prices. From there, you proceed to the payment gateway and you will get a turn in the next available time slot for the fast queue, through a QR code in "My Plans," which you'll need to show to access it. You can take a photo of the QR code to avoid searching for it individually when accessing.

  The price varies depending on the season, attendance, and attraction, so you'll see prices ranging from €5 to €18 per person. There are no child discounts; each person in the group accessing the fast queue needs their own pass, except for children under 3 years old. The €5 passes usually save little waiting time, as they are for days and attractions with medium attendance.

  Note that these Premier Access One passes sell out by time slots, and once sold out for the day, no new ones are available until the next morning. If you're unable to access it from your mobile (please check that your reservation is linked; just doing so should bring up the option), you can purchase it at City Hall in Disneyland Park or Studio Services at Walt Disney Studios.

  This is an attractive option to consider if your budget allows for it, you're in peak season, it's your last day, or you still haven't accessed the attraction you're most interested in at the park. If you decide to purchase it, do so as soon as the day begins (even from midnight onwards). If you then want to buy additional passes, for that or another attraction, it will allow you once your time slot has started, up to a maximum of 3 passes per day.

-

- **Disney Premier Access Ultimate:** This system offers a "flat rate" fast access: it consists of a paid pass per person and per day, which allows you to access each of the included attractions once, without time slots.

The price per person and day depends on the season and attendance, currently ranging from 90 to 190 €, and it is purchased through the app, website, or by phone.

The number of Premier Access Ultimate passes for sale is also **limited per day.** Once purchased, it guarantees fast access to all attractions on that date, without time slots, unless they are out of service or closed. Access is fast but not immediate, as you have to enter through the fast lane.

Does it make sense to purchase the Premier Access Ultimate? You will have to analyse your case: if it fits into the budget, if you are in high season, with French school holidays and high attendance, if you are going for a very short time or just one day to both parks, and you want to maximise the number of attractions you can experience.

Additionally, it makes sense only for adults and older children, as half of the attractions are roller coasters with height restrictions.

If you are sure about purchasing it, especially during peak season or for a single day, buy it in advance to avoid running out for that day. If you are unsure, going during medium season, or have more days to enjoy the park, there will probably be availability to purchase it during your stay.

Depending on the arrival date, and whether you purchase the Disney Premier Access Ultimate in your reservation or later, a different **cancellation policy** applies, allowing cancellation free of charge between 3 and 7 days before arrival. Don't forget to check it on the website when purchasing the pass.

Premier Access One and Premier Access Ultimate Attractions	
Disneyland Park	**Walt Disney Studios**
Big Thunder Mountain	Avengers Assemble: Flight Force
Phantom Manor	Spiderman W.E.B. Adventure
Peter Pan's Flight	Crush's Coaster
Buzz Lightyear Laser Blast	Ratatouille: The Adventure
It's a Small World!	The Twilight Zone Tower of Terror
Star Wars Hyperspace Mountain	Cars Road Trip
Autopia	
Star Tours: the Adventures continue	
Indiana Jones and the Temple of Peril	
Orbitron (only Disney Premier Access One)	
Pirates of the Caribbean	

In addition to Disney Premier Access One and Ultimate, there are other options to save you wait times: the Single Rider line, the Rider Switch option (both free), and Disney Vip Tours (paid).

Single Rider

The "Single Rider" line is a free service offered by Disneyland to reduce wait times on certain attractions. It's a special line for those who want to ride alone on attractions (ages 8 and up). For example, if a group of 3 people from the regular line wants to ride an attraction whose cars seat 4 people, the Cast Member will fill the car with a person from the Single Rider line.

It's a way to quickly bypass the queue if only one of you is riding, but it's only available on five attractions: Star Wars Hyperspace at Disneyland Park; and Crush's Coaster, RC Racer, Toy Soldiers, and Ratatouille: The Adventure at Walt Disney Studios.

Rider Switch or "Baby Switch"

It's a "turn" system for parents, available on attractions where a small child cannot ride due to height or age restrictions. You approach the regular line together and inform the Cast Member that you want to use Rider Switch (they must verify that you have a young child).

The first companion goes on the attraction with the children who can ride, and upon exit, they will be given a card for the second companion to use. The second companion enters directly through the fast lane and can be accompanied by a child. Travelling with babies may sometimes seem like "a burden" to your older children, but it's the moment to show them that thanks to the baby, they have this advantage!

Disneyland Paris tested in the past another free system that could help in such cases: the Standby Pass. Right now, it's not active, but it's possible that in the coming months testing will resume on various attractions. It consists of a virtual queue that assigns you a time slot to ride the attraction.

Disney VIP Tours

For those with more flexible budgets, there are VIP Tours available for an additional fee on top of your tickets, where a Cast Member will accompany you on a tour of the entire park for approximately 6 hours, enjoying attractions, shows, and character encounters with fast access and privileged location. Tours must be booked in advance via email by contacting dlp.viptours.experience@disney.com

Security at Disneyland Paris

Before entering the park each day, take a few minutes to review safety with your family. Each child should carry identification and, if possible, know how to show it to park employees (Cast Members). Show your children what the employees wear, the badge they carry, and what to say if they get lost. Cast Members will escort the child to the "Lost Children" area, a room with stuffed animals to make the wait less disturbing, located at the following locations:

- In Disneyland Park: between Plaza Gardens Restaurant and the first aid station.

- In Walt Disney Studios Park: at the entrance, next to Studio Services.

If you lose sight of your child, immediately **notify the nearest Cast Member,** who will activate the search protocol, and go directly to the "Lost Children" area.

Only if your child is older (teenager), you can establish a family meeting point in each land; if they're not there, notify the nearest Cast Member, who will activate the search protocol.

For identification, City Hall or Disney hotel receptions usually have bracelets to fill out with the child's information or cards to carry on a lanyard. You can also print them in advance, use a temporary tattoo, or write directly on the arm with a permanent marker.

What information to include? Of course, name, parents' or guardians' phone number, and the hotel where they are staying. It's advisable to add any allergies and blood type.

Try to have a **photo** of each child when entering the park; it will not only be a nice memory, but will also allow you to quickly show the Cast Member what colours and clothing the child is wearing, their appearance, build, and height.

Additionally, if available, children can wear a GPS position watch, activating the roaming function on their SIM with credit, or an Airtag attached to their clothing.

It sounds easy to say, but in the event a child gets lost, the key is to stay calm. These moments can happen (nothing runs as fast as a child towards their favourite character), and the most important thing is to solve them with a clear mind as soon as possible.

Cast Members are accustomed to these situations and will try to keep the child calm and entertained; they may even tell them that they are not lost, it's the adults who are lost!

Finally, in case of an accident or serious emergency, here are the phone numbers for French emergency services:

Emergency — 112
Ambulance — 15 or 112
Police — 17 or 112
Fire brigade — 18 or 112
24-hour healthcare — 01 47 07 77 77

Robberies, Thefts, and Lost items

Disneyland Paris is a very safe park, with CCTV surveillance and security personnel, both uniformed and plainclothes, at entrances and within the parks, shops, etc. However, the park does not take responsibility for thefts or losses of personal belongings, so it recommends using lockers, following their conditions of use, and keeping an eye on personal items.

Although the high price of tickets acts as a significant barrier to pickpockets and "distraction thieves," like any vacation destination, there may be isolated cases of theft, especially in areas without access control like Disney Village and the train station. We recommend exercising caution, keeping an eye on your belongings, not leaving valuable items in strollers, and wearing backpacks on the front.

It's also important to remember these tips when visiting Paris. In the metro and some tourist areas, pickpocketing groups and scammers operate with classic tricks (fake signature requests, shell games, etc.). Pay close attention at ATMs, don't leave your phone on the table at outdoor cafes, and avoid using it in the metro/train.

If, despite precautions, you have a valuable item stolen, especially personal documentation, it's advisable to follow these steps:

If you're in the park, the first step is to go to **Lost and Found Office,** located at City Hall in Disneyland Park and near Studio Services in Walt Disney Studios, or through their specific app Troov. There, you can check if any of your belongings have been turned in and leave your contact information in case they turn up later.

If you've already left the park, you can contact Lost and Found through **Troov** (an online service that works with Disneyland Paris to match items declared lost and items found in the resort) or try via email at Dlp.objets.trouves@disney.com.

Next, you should **report the loss or theft to the police**. This report will prevent your liability in case your documentation is used fraudulently and may be necessary for leaving the country. In addition, it will help you obtain a new passport or a travel document to return home and is required for claiming compensation from insurance if you have this coverage. The "Police Nationale" (police station) in Chessy is open 24 hours and is located 1 km from the park entrance, on Rue du Grand Secours, towards the Val d'Europe shopping center.

With a copy of the report, if you don't have any other documentation to travel, you should go to the consulate of your country in Paris to obtain new documentation or a travel document if your departure is imminent.

As mentioned, in addition to filing the corresponding report at the police station, as mentioned, Disneyland Paris has a specific application called Troov where you can report **lost items** in the park. The app will notify you if an object similar to yours is found.

If the loss occurs in Paris, there are several Lost and Found points where you can try to recover your lost or stolen personal items.

Firstly, the online Lost and Found office of the Paris Prefecture: http://objetstrouvesprefecturedepolice.franceobjetstrouves.fr

On their website, you can post an ad with details of your belongings and your contact information, and if someone finds them, you can retrieve them by paying an €11 handling fee and shipping costs if you want them mailed to you.

There are specific Lost and Found spots to visit if the loss occurred at the airport, train stations, or within the metro network; as well as online forms for each one of these locations.

Luggage

Your reservation and all the arrangements are ready, the trip is near, so, what do you need to bring? Throughout this section, we'll explain in detail the essentials for your suitcases and backpacks.

The list is very comprehensive; the idea is not to buy and carry everything we suggest, but to review it and personalise your own list. This will improve your trip, and leave space in the suitcase for souvenirs.

If you're travelling with a baby, those essentials multiply. In our "Travelling with Babies" section, you'll find many useful ideas to make your trip more comfortable.

The list may seem extensive, but don't worry! At the end of the guide, you'll find a summarised checklist to quickly check that you haven't forgotten anything. Before packing your suitcase (and one last time before travelling), it's advisable to review it, print reservations, check in for flights, and check the weather forecast to adapt your luggage. Don't forget to review our sections "Travelling in Bad Weather" and "Travelling in Hot Weather", if applicable.

Documents and Phone

It's advisable to carry **personal identification documents** or passports in a safe, waterproof, and easily accessible place, so you can quickly pull them out when requested. Although for travelling to France, in the case of European citizens, a national identification card is sufficient, we always travel with double identification, such as IDs and passports, stored in separate parts of our carry-on luggage, for any eventuality. Also, carry a copy of the documentation on your mobile phone, in an email addressed to yourself, or a paper photocopy stored separately.

Children travelling with their parents or guardians should also carry their documentation, including babies, as well as a copy of the documentation confirming their parentage.

If minors are travelling with people other than both parents or guardians, in order to leave certain countries, they must present a declaration of permission to travel outside the national territory, signed by both parents. This authorization can be signed at police stations.

On the day you are travelling to France your passport must meet 2 requirements. Your passport must be: Less than 10 years old on the day you enter (check the 'date of issue'); and valid for at least 3 months after the day you plan to leave (check the 'expiry date'). Full details on passport rules for travel to France can be found at:

https://www.gov.uk/foreign-travel-advice/france/entry-requirements

Check the **expiry dates** for everyone's documents, both children and adults, so that oversight doesn't ruin your trip. Don't forget student IDs or other discount cards if you plan to visit Paris; military ID if you can access discounts on tickets, and your driver's licence if renting a car.

European Health Insurance Card (EHIC): For European citizens, this card allows access to public healthcare in France under the same conditions as French citizens (with co-payment). The application for the card is free and can be requested online, and it will be delivered to your home. It's also advisable to carry a photocopy or digital copy of the children's health or vaccination records.

For UK citizens, the **UK Global Health Insurance Card (GHIC)** allows you to access healthcare in EU countries, including France, on the same basis as a resident of that country (this means, with healthcare co-payments). A UK GHIC is free and lasts for up to 5 years, and you can apply for it through the NHS website

Travel Insurance: As mentioned, the French public health system operates with co-payment, and even if you have it, the European Health Insurance Card doesn't always cover all medical expenses (tests, analysis, etc.). Therefore, it's advisable to purchase travel medical insurance covering both adults and children, and keep with you the policy or corresponding cards. There are countless insurance companies, so it's best to check with your insurer and compare to get the best price.

Cancellation Insurance: As seen in "Cancellations and Modifications," Disneyland Paris normally allows you to cancel or modify your Hotel + Tickets reservation up to 7 days before arrival, obtaining a full refund. Flights are not covered by this service, but you can purchase specific insurance for them; or even full coverage insurance for flights + accommodation, up to just before arrival, if booked through an agency.

Tickets, both outbound and return: keep them always available not only online but also offline (saved in photos or by email) in case you cannot connect to the network; and it doesn't hurt to carry a paper copy until you check in and get the boarding passes (your phone battery can die at the worst moment).

Check-in as early as possible, both outbound and return. Remember to set an alarm so you don't forget to check in for the return flight.

Reservations for tickets and accommodation, as well as any other contracted services; bring both a printed copy and another on your phone.

Phone and Portable Battery: In Disneyland, it's necessary to have a phone with battery all day long: not only will it allow you to access the App, check the map, manage reservations, or use Premier Access, but you'll also take hundreds of photos with it, so it's good to have plenty of battery and memory. Make sure to have your photos backed up in the cloud or Google Photos, and carry portable batteries to recharge your phone.

For **European citizens, roaming** (mobile network) is free in France, and there are no additional charges for browsing the App, using WhatsApp, etc. Nonetheless, check with your phone provider if you have any doubts, and connect to the free park and hotel Wi-Fi to avoid consuming data if you have limited data. For **UK citizens,** you may check with your phone provider for additional charges for roaming.

Next to Café Hyperion, in the Videopolis arcades, there's a **free charging station** where you can recharge phones or cameras, although you'll need your own cable. In the parks, there are also paid charging stations, located at the beginning of Main Street in Disneyland Park, and in Studio 1 in Walt Disney Studios. You can rent a portable battery and cable there, for both Android and Apple devices, for about €4 (2 hours) or €10 (all day), to avoid waiting while your phone charges.

You don't need to bring all cables and plugs to the parks; think about the ones you'll need. The rest, have them ready to charge devices while you sleep.

The **plugs** in the hotels are generally EU, but they also have a UK 3-pin plug, and sometimes a USB outlet (occasionally, in the television). Don't hesitate to ask reception for any adapters you may need. At the Esso gas station in front of the Santa Fe and Cheyenne hotels, they also have a wide range of adapters.

Phone case with strap, or lanyard: the first one will keep your phone always handy, avoiding having to take it out of your backpack every time to check the App, take photos, etc. Additionally, in some options, they have a small compartment where you can carry your entry ticket or Magic Pass, Photopass, and a payment card.

Another alternative, if you prefer to carry the Magic Pass and Photopass in physical rather than digital format, is the **lanyard:** these small wallets with straps that hang around your neck are another accessory in the Park (in fact, they are for sale for €15). They're even a collector's item that people decorate with commemorative pins.

Regarding **payment methods,** all shops and restaurants accept Visa, MasterCard, and American Express. Before travelling, confirm with your bank that your card allows international charges (for security, they are usually blocked, and you may not be able to use it in the park), and check with your bank if there are additional charges for transactions abroad.

If your transaction rate is high and you don't have an alternative card, you should consider paying in advance for as many services as possible, i.e., getting Meal Plans.

Until April 2024, **MasterCard** cardholders have an extra benefit, free tickets with preferred seating for several shows. We'll tell you how to get those preferred tickets in our "Shows" section in case this offer gets back.

Additionally, you can find several **ATMs,** both in Disneyland Paris and Walt Disney Studios, Disney Village, and the Marne - La Vallée train station. As fees can be very high, it's advisable to carry cash and loose change in case of any issues. It will also come handy for lockers, etc.

For visitors from outside the Eurozone, there are currency exchange points (with significant high fees/low rates) at the entrance of Disneyland Park, at City Hall, and at Studio Services, as well as at hotel receptions and at the post office in the Marne - La Vallée train station. They have limited opening hours, remember to check them in advance.

Clothing and Footwear

The most important aspect is to wear **comfortable footwear.** since you'll be walking many kilometres each day; in fact, it's ideal to bring two pairs and alternate between them. This applies to children as well—no flip-flops, light up sneakers or roller shoes, and avoid any footwear that might come off on fast rides. Also, you'll have to pay attention to both children and adults glasses on some rides, taking them off and securing them in a closed pocket.

Clothing should also be comfortable, allowing you to get on and off rides, fasten harnesses, and even ride on a carousel horse. It's best to forget about miniskirts or tight-fitting styles. The park's policy is to ask visitors to wear "family-friendly" clothing that isn't offensive in terms of messages, cleavage, etc.

You'll see many personalised shirts, bright colours and matching styles, which help children find adults in crowds, and vice versa. The weather is highly variable, so it's most important to **wear layers** that you can add or remove depending on the temperature (even in summer, it's advisable to bring a lightweight sweater for the evenings). We've prepared two special sections, **"Travelling in Cold Weather"** and **"Travelling in Hot Weather"**, with tips for dealing with different Parisian climates.

Even if the weather is hot, swimsuits or bikinis aren't worn in the park since there aren't many attractions where you can get wet (you'll find these in our "Travelling in Hot Weather" section). Don't forget your swimsuit and flip-flops if the hotel has a pool, or, in summer, if you're also visiting Paris and the Paris Plages. In some hotels and water parks, it's necessary for the swimsuit to be tight-fitting. Towel service is available at Disney hotels; it's advisable to inquire about any other accommodations. Regarding the suitcase itself, it's important that it's identified and personalised in case it gets lost.

Toiletry Bag and First Aid Kit

Regarding the toiletry bag, remember to bring all the products you usually need, with special attention to airline regulations regarding liquids in carry-on luggage (which will change as of 2025) and prohibited products onboard. One detail is that chewing gum isn't sold in the parks due to maintenance reasons, but it's not prohibited to bring it.

With regard to the first aid kit, having medications and pharmacy items will alleviate symptoms if any of you get sick. Fatigue, temperature changes on planes and in restaurants, meals, etc., can take a toll on anyone's health; a good first aid kit will make your trip more bearable, and "prevention is better than cure." In all cases, bring the appropriate medications for each child or adult, according to your doctor's instructions.

These are the most general medications for a basic first aid kit:

- Thermometer
- Pain relievers / antipyretics / anti-inflammatories
- Plasters/band-aid's, Compeed blister care, anti-chafing stick
- Chlorhexidine, arnica stick, gauze pads, and saline solution in single-dose packets
- Sea sickness pills
- Cold and antihistamine medication, throat lozenges
- Allergy medication, as prescribed by a doctor
- Antacid, laxative, antidiarrheal, probiotic, and oral rehydration solution (for children and adults)
- Contact lens solution / spare glasses / dental splint
- Sunscreen, After Sun lotion, mosquito repellent, and Afterbite (in summer)
- Lip balm
- Hand sanitizer spray or gel, wipes, and tissues

To adapt this list to your family, consider the common or recurring illnesses of each member: diabetes, allergies, intolerances, otitis, cystitis, cold sores, etc. Check with your doctor and pharmacist if you need any additional prescriptions for these cases, or to carry liquids of more than 100 ml in your suitcase.

If your children are particularly active, for example, consider carrying wound closure strips and specific treatments for bumps or wounds.

If you need any other first aid items during your trip, in our "First Aid" section you'll find the location of the nearest first aid stations, pharmacies, and convenience points.

Backpack

Choose simple and compact backpacks with few compartments to facilitate passing through the access control. When getting on the attractions, you'll carry the backpack with you; if the ride is intense, place it between your legs passing the straps around them.

Be careful to close it securely (both yours and your children's), as you wouldn't want wallets or cameras flying, especially on Tower of Terror (bear in mind the kids' glasses, as well). In some attractions like RC Racer and Parachute Drop, the backpack is left in compartments until the exit. If you don't want to carry it all day, you can leave it in lockers for about €7.

Try to make sure the backpacks are waterproof or use a waterproof spray. On days of heavy rain, it will help keep your belongings dry, both when placing it on the ground in the attractions and if you're not wearing a poncho.

Remember not to carry in it objects considered "dangerous" according to park regulations, such as sharp objects, selfie sticks, etc.

Water bottle: Tap water is free at Disneyland Paris, while small bottles of mineral water cost around €4. Bring your own filled bottle to refill at the park's drinking water fountains. The best option is an aluminium one (Chilly's bottles retain cold better) or collapsible to save space.

If you're concerned about the taste of tap water, there are bottles with built-in filters, like Brita or Philips, costing around €15. Just bring one and distribute the water to others once filtered.

Some families even bring Kool-Aid packets to turn the water into a soft drink instantly. Restaurants are required to serve it for free, just ask for "un pichet d'eau" or "une carafe d'eau," and if it's hot, "un verre avec de la glace."

Finally, you'll find bottled mineral water at a better price at the Esso service area or train station, along with juices and other products to take to the park. You can find all the information in our dining section.

Snacks: Early mornings and waiting times will make you hungry, both children and adults! Although the park is full of tempting treats, there's hardly anything healthy, and the prices aren't cheap, so by the end of the trip, they'd add up. Carry snack bags in your backpack; the options are endless, more or less healthy.

You can opt for fruit, raisins, Babybel cheeses, fruit pouches (treat them like liquids for the plane), and cereal bars; but also chips or chocolates, which are outrageously expensive in the park (take a look at our Kiosks section in Restaurants). Avoid whole nuts, popcorn, cherry tomatoes, whole grapes, and any other food that children can choke on.

If you want to bring your own food to the park, opt for an insulated bag (hard plastic coolers are not allowed), containers not made of glass (except for documented allergies or intolerances, you should bring simple foods), and not overly sharp cutlery, to pass through the access control safely.

Costumes and Accessories

Mickey and Minnie Ears: These are the go-to accessory in the park, for both kids and adults! It's best to bring them in advance since the ones sold in the park are quite expensive (there are various price ranges, but many cost around €35), and this way, you'll have them for the first photos. You can find them in many stores, from Amazon to H&M or Primark. The official Disney Store website often has good deals when discontinuing a limited edition. To attach them to your backpack, the most practical option is a "slap band"; customised Disney ones (or "cutie cuff") are the latest trend in American parks.

If your kids are young, they'll enjoy wearing a **costume** of their favourite character, and in certain attractions, if the kids are dressed as the theme of the attraction, the whole family is allowed to access through the fast lane (this is at the discretion of the Cast Member, not a right, and depends on the attraction's crowd).

There are options for all tastes: Peter Pan and Tinkerbell or Wendy; Buzz Lightyear in Toy Story attractions; Pirates, Indiana Jones, Star Wars characters, Avengers, superheroes, or even Chef Linguini — let your imagination run wild! Unfortunately, it doesn't work in the Princess Pavilion, mostly because half of it is already in costume!

Even in the Frozen Sing Along show, girls dressed as Elsa get a special spot and one, chosen at random, gets to go on stage!

As mentioned, this is a "gift" and not a requirement from the park; nevertheless, dressing up will make them have a great time, and in many cases, it's the magical touch they need, for example, to make interactions more fun if they meet their favourite character.

It's also a good idea to bring costumes from home, although the park has options for all tastes (spectacular ones cost around €50). As mentioned in the Accommodation section, the renovated Disneyland Hotel offers the "My Royal Dream" service, a fairy tale transformation with makeup, hairstyle, and even costumes, with different prices and extras depending on the package chosen.

The experience can be added as an extra to your reservation at a Disney hotel. However, there are always more budget-friendly options: in Fantasyland and Studio 1 at Walt Disney Studios, there are **face painting** services for around €10; or you can also bring some glitter, rhinestones, paints (even fluorescent ones) to create your own magic.

From the age of 12, you cannot enter the park dressed in a costume (except for special parties or events like Halloween); this is to avoid confusion with other visitors about the characters. What is allowed is **"Disney bounding"**, dressing inspired by the character of your choice, with their colour combination or accessories, and more and more examples are seen in Disneyland Paris, as well as Disney shirts, etc. In this regard, it's important that those over 12 are not mistaken for characters: they cannot sign autographs or pretend to be them, and for safety reasons, dresses cannot drag on the ground, etc.

Remember to bring an **autograph book**; they're quite expensive in the park, and their pens run out quickly! In our "Characters" section, you'll see ideas for getting the best signature from your favourite character.

Luggage Storage and Disney Express Service

If you arrive at Disneyland Paris early and want to go directly to the parks or want to enjoy them until the very last minute of your last day, there are several options for luggage storage: at the hotels, at the station, and even in the park itself. Additionally, the Disney Express service can transport your luggage to and from your hotels, as you'll see below.

You cannot enter the parks with bags larger than 55 cm x 40 cm x 25 cm, but in the consignment areas, you can leave luggage of almost any size, or even shopping bags, if you don't want to use the Disney Shopping Service.

Hotel Guest Storage

All Disney hotels and partner hotels (except Davy Crockett Ranch) offer free luggage storage, accessible 24 hours a day, usually located near the reception desk (follow signs for "Bagagerie"). The service varies in each hotel; for example, at Hotel Campanile Val de France, the consignment room has large lockers with electronic locks where you can store your luggage personally.

Guest Storage at Disneyland Park and Walt Disney Studios

At the entrances of both parks, there are consignment areas where you can leave your luggage. The office opens every day at 8 a.m. and closes 45 minutes after the parks' closing time.

When depositing your luggage, you can confirm the day's schedule on the board next to the office.

- In Disneyland Park, the consignment area is open year-round and is located to the right of the entrance next to Guest Relations.

- In Walt Disney Studios, the consignment area may be closed during low season. You'll find it to the right of the ticket sales lockers.

The staff will ask you to open your bags to check for any dangerous or prohibited items. Consignment prices vary from €4 for small items to €15 for large items and can be paid in cash or by card. Inform the Cast Member if your luggage is fragile so they can handle it with care, and remember that food and drink are not allowed in the consignment area.

Luggage Storage at the Train Station

There is a luggage storage service at Marne - La Vallée train station, open from 7 a.m. to 10 p.m. It's advisable to confirm the opening hours as they vary by season, depending on the park's schedule.

The storage area is on the first mezzanine floor of the station building, up the stairs from the main hall. To deposit your luggage, you must pass through a security check, where they will ensure that no food or computers are left behind. Prices for lockers range from €5 to €10, depending on their size, and are slightly more expensive than those in the park and hotels, although it can be very convenient if you need to catch a train on the last day. It's advisable to bring coins as you need to pay for lockers in cash.

Disney Express Check-In & Luggage Service

The Marne - La Vallée - Chessy station is right in front of the entrances to both Disney parks, so you may not want to waste time going to the hotel to drop off your luggage, check-in, collect tickets, and return to the park.

The Disney Express service allows you to pre-check-in at your hotel at their counter, collect tickets, and go directly to the park while they take your luggage to the hotel. Likewise, on the day of departure, they will transfer your luggage from the hotel to the station, saving you that trip while you enjoy the parks for as long as possible.

The service costs €17 per person (except for children under 3), includes "round trip," and is available to guests of all Disney hotels and partner hotels, except Disney's Davy Crockett Ranch and Villages Nature Paris.

How to Book Disney Express Service?

You can book Disney Express on the website as part of your package reservation or add it later; through your travel agency; or by contacting their call center (local call rate, consider using Skype for cheaper calls).

How Does the Service Work?

On the day of arrival: Disney Express takes care of your luggage from the moment you arrive at the Disney Express counter at Marne la Vallée/Chessy station. Head to the first-floor mezzanine of the station, where you'll see blue signs pointing to the Disney Express counter (different from the station's own consignment), open from 7:45 a.m. to 9 p.m., every day of the week.

Once there, a staff member will provide you with the necessary documentation to check in at the hotel, your park tickets, and if you're staying at a Disney hotel, the Magic Pass, which also serves as the room key. Deposit your luggage, properly identified, and start enjoying the park without going to the hotel. For security reasons, the Disney Express counter does not accept certain objects, such as jewellery, laptops, cameras, baby strollers, or golf clubs...

On the day of departure, simply leave your luggage at the consignment area of your hotel before 11 a.m. Disney Express will take care of sending your luggage to Marne la Vallée/Chessy station, so you can enjoy the last moments of magic in peace. When leaving the park, you only have to pick up your luggage at the Disney Express counter at the station, between 1 p.m. and 9 p.m., making sure to pick it up 45 minutes before your train departure.

When Is Disney Express Service Worth It?

If it fits your budget, there are situations where the expense of hiring this service is worthwhile:

- If you want to quickly head to the parks but are travelling with very young children or elderly people, you'll save them a long journey.

- If you're travelling with a lot of luggage (since the price is per person), or if you have very little time and want to maximise your time in the park on the day of arrival and departure.

- If you're staying at a partner hotel, as they are further from the park, the cost of Disney Express may be an interesting option.

When Is It Not Worth It to Hire Disney Express?

In addition to being expensive, there are situations where the expense of Disney Express is not worthwhile:

- If you're in a very large group: the Disney Express rate is per person and not per item, and it can be very expensive overall.

- Similarly, it's not worth it if you're travelling with little luggage and can manage the hotel arrival well, or if you want to take the opportunity to freshen up before going to the parks.

- Finally, if your hotel is very close to the entrances and the station, such as the New York Marvel, it's usually worth making the trip and check-in in person.

Disneyland App: Maps and Programs

Since September 2022, Disneyland Paris no longer offers paper maps and programs; instead, all this information is at your fingertips in the park's app, available for iPhone and Android. In it, you will have the park map, attraction wait times, information about restaurants, your tickets, and Magic Pass, etc.

Additionally, through the app, you can book spots at shows (for an extra fee), tables at various restaurants, and slots for meetings with superheroes at the Hero Training Centre in Walt Disney Studios.

It's best to try the app before your trip (it's available on Google Play and the App Store) to understand how it works: how to view the map, how to order food in advance (we explain this in our Restaurants section).

Also, by linking your reservation number in the app or scanning the ticket with your phone, you can see all the information about your trip, add services like Disney Premier Access, or make reservations at table-service restaurants and buffets.

The **interactive map** feature of the app is the best way to navigate the parks. It shows the location of information points, Baby Care Centers (don't miss our "Travelling with Babies" section about these points), or restrooms.

The most used feature is the interactive attraction map, which shows the location of each one, wait times, show schedules, or any service interruptions. With it, you can plan your visit and adapt to each moment. To go directly to what interests you, filter by park, interests, or age and height restrictions.

A tip to avoid constantly navigating through the long list of Disneyland Paris attractions is to add your preferred ones to the favourites section. You'll receive quick alerts about your favourite attractions and have a small list to see their wait times in the days prior.

There's also a complementary app, **Magipark App**. With the "Live" feature of this unofficial app on your phone, you can add your 8 favourite attractions and see real wait times on the lock screen. Additionally, you'll receive a notification if a ride's service is interrupted or if its wait time reaches a certain interval, and, as a novelty, it includes wait times for Single Rider lines and Extra Magic Time.

Check-In

An important feature of the official Disneyland Paris app allows you to save time at check-in at Disney hotels. From the app, with your session started and the reservation linked in "My Hotel Reservations," you can start check-in 7 days before your arrival.

Moreover, with the introduction in 2024 of the digital Magic Pass, you only need to leave your luggage in storage (or in your vehicle) and head to the park, even taking advantage of Extra Magic Time. Thus, you'll only need to pick up the physical Magic Pass (your room access card) at the hotel reception when you go there to rest.

As an alternative, you can provide the printed personal information form (one per traveller) when checking in, printing the form available on the park's website.

When the room is ready, usually from 3 p.m., you'll receive an SMS or email with its number, so you can access it upon return using the Magic Pass as the room key.

This early check-in is especially useful if you decide to spend the previous night in another accommodation, check into the Disney hotel early in the morning, and go directly to the park to enjoy Extra Magic Time.

A practical and quick solution for that previous night, especially when travelling with young children, is to leave the luggage at the hotel's storage and bring only one bag with a change of clothes per person; it will save you time and facilitate your entrances and exits.

Check-Out

Check-out at Disney hotels, in general, is before 11 a.m. It's very simple since you only need to leave the room before that time. From 11 a.m., the key and the hotel bill are deactivated.

Your Magic Pass will still work as an entry to Disneyland Paris, so you can leave your luggage in storage and go to the park, and you'll continue to have free parking during the day. As an exception, the Davy Crockett Ranch does not have its own storage, and you must deposit the room keys in a mailbox.

Language

In Disneyland Paris, two languages coexist, French and English (although more than a third of the Cast Members also speak another language, such as Spanish or German). Each worker wears little flags on their identification with the languages they speak.

All restaurant menus have a QR code, with which you can access the menu version in your language. Regarding attractions, some have dialogues in French and others in English; the clue to know which language prevails is in the name of each one (thus, the Genie's directions as "film director" are in French in the Flying Carpets attraction, "les Tapis Volants").

Most shows mix both languages, although generally, the dialogues are minimal (except in Stitch live!) and focus more on gestures and music. In the Mickey and the Magician show, for example, Mickey speaks in French and the other characters in English.

As a curiosity, Disney's agreements with the French government for the creation of the park included that some attractions should be in French, and that the French anthem, La Marseillaise, should be heard in the park (in Liberty Arcade, specifically, where you'll find a hidden passage, behind the Statue of Liberty painting).

During the Trip

Finally, the day has arrived, welcome to Disneyland Paris! Throughout the following pages, we will reveal all the secrets to enjoying your visit to the fullest.

Access to the Park

The fastest way to pass through the **access control** is to be well prepared for it, almost like when we're about to board a plane! Try to access the queues at the sides, mainly on the left. 80% of the population is right-handed and tends to choose the right side, so applying this logic to any queue in the park (such as when the queue for Big Thunder Mountain splits in two), you can save precious minutes.

Carry what you'll need for the day in simple backpacks, without many compartments to check. Keep any metallic items (phone, keys, coins) separated. Remember not to bring prohibited items, such as any toy that may resemble a weapon, balls, selfie sticks, or glass containers, except for baby food or bottles.

Regarding exit and re-entry: if you wish to leave one of the Parks and be readmitted later on the same day, you should approach an employee before exiting the turnstiles to ensure you have all the necessary elements for your readmission (tickets, stamps, etc.).

Lands and Attractions

Disneyland Paris is not as large nor does it have as many attractions as other Disney parks, but it is possibly the most beautiful of them all. When creating the Paris park, Disney set a very high standard to create a place of fantasy on the continent where most classic fairy tales take place, which, combined with the experience gained in other parks, resulted in a picturesque architecture.

Throughout this chapter, we will review the history and curiosities of each territory or land and its attractions, and at the end of the guide, you will find our summary table with all the information about them: if they open during Extra Magic Time or allow Disney Premier Access, if they have any age or height restrictions, if they are suitable for pregnant women, etc.

Disneyland Park

As mentioned, Disneyland Park consists of 5 Lands or areas, inspired by the world of fantasy, adventures, and discoveries, and dedicated to the great classics of animation and the spirit of Disney's early theme parks.

Main Street, U.S.A.

Inspired by an American avenue from the early 20th century, this main street welcomes park visitors and leads them straight to the Castle. The low roofs and forced perspective of the street magnify the impression upon entering, as a visual trick that makes the street seem longer and the Castle larger and farther away than it actually is.

The experience that Imagineers sought to create on Main Street was that of a "real" street, with inhabitants and customers, so sounds reinforcing that sensation can be heard, such as piano lessons, sounds from the dentist's office, etc.

Additionally, these shops are filled with a "Disney" sense of humour: on the first floor of Bixby Brothers, an owl announces a sleepwalker's club; in another window, a dinosaur represents a society of palaeontologists... In another corner is the "Kitty Hawk" store whose owners, the Wright brothers, "have gone out for flight practice," and if you look at the sign with the giant cup, you'll see that it's so hot that "it's smoking."

City Hall: as its name implies, this is the "City Hall" of the park. The place to go should you have any problem with reservations, claims and complaints, but also to add extras to your trip, listen to Mickey's free congratulatory call (don't miss our "Celebrating a Birthday" section), thank a Cast Member for their work, or get special MasterCard tickets for shows. This point has its equivalent in Walt Disney Studios, called Studio Services and is also located at the park entrance.

The place is picturesque, decorated with a giant map of the resort and the first "concept art" of the park. You can also find different memories, such as pictures of Walt Disney receiving the French Legion of Honour. As a sample of Disney humour, there is a plaque here inviting "lost parents" to wait there for their children, but be careful, only "lost parents"! Children should always go to the Baby Center Meeting Point.

The history of Main Street U.S.A. is that of an American city from 1890 to 1920, where horse-drawn carriages are progressively giving way to classic cars and the railroad, which is why the two main attractions in this land are to ride aboard these means of transportation:

On one hand, **"Disney Railroad"** is the steam railway line that runs along the perimeter of Disneyland Park. Upon entering the park, you'll pass under the Main Street train station, where you can take the train that will take you through the different lands (although some stops may be closed) to the Fantasyland stop, next to the Meet Mickey dressing room.

On the other hand, the **"Horse-Drawn Streetcars"** consist of omnibuses that run on rails, guided by horses on a predetermined circuit.

And finally, the **"Main Street Vehicles",** a fleet of classic vehicles from the early 20th century, such as a fire truck or the Double Decker Bus. The stop is to the right of Town Square, the central square of Main Street with its unmistakable kiosk.

Fantasyland

From Town Square, and passing through the Castle, we arrive at Fantasyland, the area dedicated to fairy tales and Disney classics, and the most magical for children. The cottages, attractions, and shops represent different European areas in small groups, such as France, the Netherlands (the Old Mill), England (Peter Pan), Italy (Bella Notte Pizzeria), or Germany (Au Chalet de la Marionette's), and all this culminates in It's a Small World!, which brings together all the cultures of the world.

The atmosphere has been very carefully crafted and includes not only attractions and restaurants but also many special sets, from King Arthur's sword to Cinderella's carriage. Check out our "Best Photos" section so you don't miss a detail!

Sleeping Beauty Castle

It's the most recognizable feature of Disney parks, but not all castles in the parks are the same; in fact, the one at Disneyland Paris is the most beautiful of all! Standing at over 40 metres tall, it maintains several elements from the movie, such as the interplay of pink and blue colours, or the square trees.

It was specially designed with architectural details from France, like its structure reminiscent of Mont Saint-Michel, the miniatures, the tiles, its gardens, and even the snails on the domes, a nod to French gastronomy. Did you know its pink hues were specifically designed to contrast with the often grey Parisian sky, unlike the sunny days in California and Florida?

At Disneyland Paris, you can visit the top of the castle by touring the Sleeping Beauty Gallery. It tells the story of Aurora through a series of stained-glass windows depicting scenes from the movie, supervised by the craftsman who worked on the reconstruction of Notre-Dame. Walk through the gallery clockwise to see them, and visit the balcony for the best views of Fantasyland and the castle towers.

The interior is equally well-maintained, so each time you walk through it, you'll notice new details, from the columns ending like tree cups to the book that starts the movie. Above the tapestry of Sleeping Aurora (which glows periodically) there is a beautiful changing stained-glass window.

The armour snores because of the spell, and the argument between Flora and Merryweather has left them pink and blue - take a flash photo of them! Next to the armour, Maleficent's crow, turned to stone, resists the enchantment; If you use the flash on your camera, it will show its red eyes!

A little-known detail is that the castle holds the "Disney family crest" on its walls, in a stone arch near the Seven Dwarfs shop. In that area, you can hear Snow White singing. Also on the right side, where you'll find the "Wishing Well". Toss a coin and make your wishes; all coins are donated to the "Make-a-Wish" charity at the end of the year.

Don't miss our tips in the **Best Photos section**, with the best spots to take your photos with the Castle in the background.

Dragon's Lair (La Tanière du Dragon): this enormous animatronic is exclusive to Disneyland Paris. With about 25 meters long and two and a half tons in weight, it was created by Imagineer Terri Hardin to inhabit this dungeon. There are several entrances to his cave; the main one is located to the left of the Castle, but it is also accessed from the back door of Merlin the Enchanter's shop, or next to the Seven Dwarfs shop.

The dungeon is dark, and the dragon is impressive (it wakes up, roars, and smokes every so often), so it can scare young children. Essential for fans of epic adventures and fantasy. It usually doesn't have an entrance queue, except for moments close to parades when more people approach the Castle, and access closes early.

Peter Pan's Flight: one of the most successful attractions in the park! In this 3-minute ride, you'll board a small pirate ship to visit the most beautiful scenes from the movie, including a flight over London with its smoking chimneys (what do you see in Big Ben's clock?). Every detail is taken care of, even the toys of the Darling children are antiques, and Peter Pan's book is an original edition by J.M. Barrie.

It's the busiest in Fantasyland, so use all possible tricks to reduce the queue time, but don't miss it; it's worth it and will delight both children and adults alike.

Lancelot's Carousel: this classic carousel is impressive, with its 86 horses and carts of various sizes, the largest on the outside and the smallest inside. It is inspired by the legends of King Arthur and his knights, hence the "round" structure of the carousel and the mediaeval armour that adorns the horses on the outside, the most impressive ones. The duration of the attraction is 2 minutes, and certain safety measures must be followed. Babies must be seated in the carriages, and children up to 3 years old or those who do not reach the footrests on the horses must be accompanied by a standing adult.

Mad Hatter's Tea Cups: The Mad Hatter's teacup ride is a park classic. This carousel has 18 cups that spin on a tray, and on themselves, thanks to a wheel with which you will handle the speed and direction of the spin of your cup (the fastest ones are the mauve ones!). The ride lasts 2 minutes, and up to 4 people can ride per cup. It's one of the prettiest in the park, with its modernist glass dome, hanging Japanese lantern lamps (don't miss it at night; it's magical), its control cabin shaped like a sugar cube, or the teapot through which the Dormouse peeks.

Alice's Curious Labyrinth: this attraction, exclusive to Disneyland Paris, consists of a hedge maze in the shape of the famous Cheshire Cat, going through different scenes from Wonderland until you reach the Queen's Castle. It's a good option during peak times because it usually doesn't have long queues and takes about 15-20 minutes to go through.

It's full of details, from the water jets that jump over your heads to the increasingly smaller doors; and in it, you'll see the Caterpillar, the Dodo (attention, it can be turned upside down), the screaming Queen... Climbing the Castle, you'll have a great view of Fantasyland and some "crazy" mirrors, but to do that, you have to avoid getting lost in the 8 dead ends of this Labyrinth. Will you make it? If you're short on time (or don't like getting lost), on days with low attendance, you can access the Queen's Castle directly from the maze exit.

Dumbo the Flying Elephant: a beautiful carousel where you'll ride small flying elephants, which you can make go up or down with a small control inside. The ride lasts about 2 minutes; if you raise the elephant, you'll have a good view of Fantasyland. Each little elephant can fly with a maximum of 2 adults and 1 child, and children must be accompanied by an adult. Adorable and perfect for small children (who don't suffer from motion sickness).

It's a Small World!: one of the most classic attractions at Disney parks, created in honour of Unicef for the 1964 New York World's Fair and designed by Mary Blair, creator of the art of Peter Pan and Alice. You'll embark on a peaceful boat ride, about 10 minutes long.

Over 300 child animatronics, characterised from all over the world, sing and dance to the catchiest melody in the park, in the language of each area you pass through. It's an endearing ride that will delight even the youngest children.

Additionally, from the outside, every quarter of an hour, you'll see a group of characters peeking out of the clock on its facade. As a curiosity, in the Hong Kong version, this attraction incorporates Elsa and Anna's animatronics, and perhaps they will be part of the French cast soon.

Storybook Land Canal Boats: a relaxed boat ride through Storybook Land, full of models of classic tales (Belle's village, Aladdin's cave, Rapunzel's tower...), where even the names of the boats are personalised (each one is a princess). The ride lasts about 6 minutes, is suitable for babies and young children, and usually has low attendance.

Throughout 2024, two new scenes will be added to this attraction, one corresponding to the Hundred Acre Wood from Winnie the Pooh, and another belonging to the Kingdom of Arendelle from Frozen, which will replace Peter and the Wolf and Hansel and Gretel, to better reflect the tales brought to the screen by Disney. The attraction will close for this renovation from March 11, 2024, and the reopening date is pending confirmation.

Casey Jr. Le Petit Train du Cirque: offers another view of Storybook Land, this time on a 2-minute journey aboard Dumbo's train. It's a good option to try for the first time with very young children and see how they adapt to a slightly faster pace.

Snow White and the Seven Dwarfs: on this journey aboard the dwarfs' mine wagons (each with its name), lasting 2 minutes, we will go through the scenes of Disney's first feature film, starting from the Queen's castle. In the queue, you can see the book with the recipe for the poisoned apple, which turns into a skull.

Be aware that our "little dwarfs" can be scared by various scenes, such as the trees in the forest or the witch's transformation. Speaking of the Evil Queen, from the outside, you can see her peering out of one of the towers, through a stained glass window.

Les Voyages de Pinocchio's: a journey through the scenes of the famous Disney classic. Although at first glance, it could be a family-friendly and gentle attraction for the little ones, it also has a gloomy side since the ride in its wagons, lasting 2 minutes, is very dark and represents some dim scenes of the movie, like the whale or Pinocchio transformed into a donkey. Small children may get scared, so it's almost never crowded. It borders two lands, Fantasyland and Adventureland, which makes sense since the story itself has both fairy tale and sea adventure elements.

Adventureland

This land is the territory dedicated to adventures and great journeys, which will enchant both big and small explorers. It has two different entrances:

The first of them, next to the Peter Pan attraction in Fantasyland and the Chalet de la Marionnette, is the gateway to the jungle of this land, which will take you directly to its main attraction, Pirates of the Caribbean.

Pirates of the Caribbean: Many attractions in the park were based on movies, but in this case, it was the other way around, and the attraction itself inspired the famous Pirates of the Caribbean saga. After becoming a blockbuster, several of its characters were incorporated, such as Captain Barbossa or even Jack Sparrow himself (Johnny Depp occasionally replaced the California animatronic, shocking visitors). Located in an old fort, you need to keep your eyes wide open because the set is full of details, and the first "Jack" is hidden. The ride is dark, with storm effects, and has two rapid descents. It's worth considering whether our children are very young or easily frightened, as it lasts about 10 minutes, which is a long time if they have a bad time.

Indiana Jones and the Temple of Peril: A roller coaster inspired by the adventures of the famous archaeologist, where you will venture, aboard some mine carts, into lost ruins in the jungle. The minimum height to access is 1.40 m. The best seats are in the front row, where you'll have the sensation of "diving" into the depths of the Hindu temple, and where the loop is most impressive. The journey lasts approximately 1 minute 30 seconds, and along the queue, you'll see a camp of shops; look for Indy's hat and whip! This attraction was "temporary," intended to entertain visitors until the opening of Space Mountain, and was supposed to be dismantled afterward, but its popularity made it stay in the park.

Adventure Island is an area of islands surrounded by a lake, perfect for exploring if you have time, especially during peak hours of attraction, as it's usually quiet. It has many elements, from Skull Rock and the Pirate Galleon to the Robinson's Cabin, all connected by hanging bridges and underground caves where a hidden treasure is rumoured to be.

Pirate Galleon and Skull Rock: These two elements were brought from Disneyland California as a gift for the Paris park. You can enter the interior of the Skull Rock, even climb to look through its eyes (remember to take a photo with flash inside the caves). It has a small waterfall that flows into the lagoon, which freezes in winter. Also, during the Halloween season, there is a show with projections that "bring to life" the enormous skull. The Pirate Galleon is currently closed indefinitely due to capacity control and the need for Cast Members' supervision to prevent damage or incidents.

Robinson's Treehouse (La Cabane des Robinson): For little explorers needing to burn off energy, a good idea is to climb the 60 steps of this enormous tree, inspired by the movie "Swiss Family Robinson", with its rooms, piano, and even a pantry. From the top of the tree, you can see the entire Adventureland area, including the boat on which they arrived at the island, and beneath it, there are hidden caves called "Le Ventre de la Terre" (The Belly of the Earth).

It is not a crowded place most of the time, and it's a good option before the French mealtime, when queues in most attractions grow significantly. Plus, kids will love crossing the impressive suspension bridge and using the tree's binoculars to see the characters from "UP", Russell and Mr. Fredricksen, between the cabin and Colonel Hathi's Pizza Outpost.

As we mentioned, Adventureland has two entrances; thus, from Castle Square, the adventure begins in an Oriental Bazaar accessed through an arch. On the walls, to the left, you'll see a huge Roc egg (although Sinbad doesn't have a Disney movie, the whole area breathes its spirit, and that of the Arabian Nights), and in the bazaar, you can find several restaurants and shops, as well as the next attraction.

Aladdin's Enchanted Passage: A walking tour surrounded by small models of different scenes from the Aladdin movie. It's not essential, but during high queues or bad weather, it's a quiet and sheltered place.

Frontierland

This area is dedicated to the American Old West, with its cowboys and gold rush, and it's the only one in the park that has its own story as a guiding thread, linking all the attractions, restaurants, and shops.

Legend has it that at the foot of a mountain in the wild American West, there was a rich and fertile valley called Thunder Mesa. It was inhabited by native tribes who worshipped the "spirit of thunder" or "Thunderbird", the mountain's protective lord. When gold was discovered there, the Big Thunder Mining Company began exploiting the veins, filling the town with settlers and irritating the spirit of thunder. The mine owner, Henry Ravenswood, built the Ravenswood mansion with the huge profits extracted from the mine, now called Phantom Manor due to the following series of catastrophic mishaps...

The city continued to grow rapidly, and with it came the railroad and steamboats (like the Molly Brown, named after the feistiest traveller on the Titanic). It became home to more and more "lost souls" and fortune seekers who only wanted to make quick money, as happened to Diamond Lil, a dancer who founded the Lucky Nugget Saloon when she found a gold nugget.

The "apple of the eye" of the evil landowner was his daughter, Melanie Ravenswood, whom he kept out of reach of any suitor who dared to approach the Phantom Manor gardens; in fact, there was no evidence, but no doubts either, that Mr. Ravenswood was behind the tragic disappearance of four such suitors.

While the landowner tried to get rid of the umpteenth suitor, a railroad engineer who wanted to elope with his daughter, the "Spirit of Thunder", long annoyed, decided to awaken and send an earthquake, which collapsed the mines and several buildings, resulting in the Ravenswood couple's death.

It is said that Mr. Ravenswood's ghost returned to get rid of the engineer and thwart Melanie's wedding, leaving her "high and dry", and since then, she has wandered the mansion dressed as a bride with her candelabra in hand. The ghost and his friends, meanwhile, populate the mansion's rooms and devote themselves to scaring anyone who dares to disturb them.

After the decline of the mine and the Ravenswood family, the cowboys and ranchers returned, bringing a quieter climate, reflected in the Cowboy Cookout Barbecue Restaurant.

Big Thunder Mountain (BTM): It is the main attraction of this land, and one of the best in the park: a roller coaster that will take you through the mine to an island located in the central lake. The best seats are in the front row, for the views, and in the last row, at the end of the train, where the "whip effect" is greater.

The journey lasts about 4 minutes and is not excessively strong (the maximum speed is 50 km/hour). To access it, you must measure at least 1.02 m. It's a lot of fun, with dramatic moments like the descent into the mine, where you can hear the miners pick, or when the car grazes the water and splashes!

Big Thunder Mountain is one of the attractions with the most service interruptions, as well as a large influx. It's advisable to visit it first thing in the morning, even using Extra Magic Time, or use Disney Premier Access later. Keep an eye on the waiting times in the app, and if you see a chance, head directly to it.

If you've already seen the night-time show, a great idea is to go to the BTM queue five minutes before the park closes. You'll have a minimal wait, and you'll experience the most magical BTM experience, with the sky illuminated by fireworks.

Phantom Manor: This old mansion populated by spirits opens its doors to visitors for an experience as eerie... as it is fun! It's a family-friendly attraction, not a "haunted house" in the traditional sense, as there are no sudden scares or physical contact with the "residents".

It's full of details and special effects: paintings that transform, faces that appear in mirrors, and clues about what happened in the Mansion and the identities of its ghosts. From the outside, the mansion itself gives us some clues about what it holds inside, like the right window, which constantly beats; or the ghosts that peek out... Once inside, we'll access an elevator full of secrets, and from there to some carts that will guide us through all the attraction's scenes. (Duration: approx. 7 minutes.)

Boot Hill Cemetery: Located at the exit of Phantom Manor, it's worth taking a stroll through it, listening to the sounds of the graves (some still beating!) and taking a look at their inscriptions, which have a somewhat dark but very amusing humour. You'll find the Ravenswood couple, who have finally stopped arguing and "in silence are together beyond this life", accompanied by two of their servants, the one who "Made the master happy" and the one who "Made the master happier". Don't miss the love triangle of the Ballards or Dakota Dick, also in that line, or the "food chain" of the squirrel, the cat, the hunter... and the bear.

Thunder Mesa Riverboat Landing: This attraction consists of a 15-minute cruise on the Frontierland lake, aboard two steamboats inspired by those that crossed the Mississippi. The first is the Mark Twain, in honour of the writer of Tom Sawyer's adventures, while the second is named after the "unsinkable" Molly Brown, who survived the sinking of the Titanic in 1912, and there are even objects from the famous American lady on one of its shelves.

Frontierland Playground: This play area (formerly known as Pocahontas Indian Village) is full of swings and slides where children (especially from 4 to 8 years old) can climb and have fun. Sometimes we forget that the little ones are not used to the dynamics of attractions and queues, and since they can't run in the park, this is a good solution for them to burn off energy for a while.

Rustler Roundup Shootin' Gallery is an electronic shooting gallery where you can test your aim, achieving a series of effects on the targets. It's the only attraction in the park with an extra cost, €2 per game and person, not included in the entrance fee, and it's optional unless you're very fond of shooting... or rivalry!

Discoveryland

The territory of discoveries, of the universe and science; which initially paid tribute to the future imagined by Jules Verne. Although this influence is gradually fading in favour of other concepts like Star Wars and Buzz Lightyear, there are still elements of this aesthetic in some attractions.

Hyperspace Mountain: The most "recycled" roller coaster was born as a tribute to the novels of Jules Verne, under the name Discovery Mountain; if you pay attention, you will see part of the original sets and logos. After successive updates, the experience is now a Star Wars adventure, where you will travel through space at breakneck speed. It's a good option if the weather is bad since both the attraction and the (long) indoor queue are covered. The duration is just over 2 minutes, and a minimum height of 1.20 m is required to ride.

Star Tours: A must for Star Wars saga fans. On this simulator ride, you will experience a galactic adventure. The queue is fully themed around the saga, with R2D2 and C-3PO inspecting the ships that will take you on a thrilling escape from the Empire, "Disney / Star Wars / Indiana Jones" luggage on the scanner, and coded messages over the loudspeakers like "Mr. Han Ford, veuillez rejoindre votre groupe" (Mr. Han Ford, please join your group). And don't miss the "Mon Calamari" in the control room!

The adventure is in 3D and features images from the entire film saga, from the oldest to the newest, in different mission combinations, making each trip, about 5 minutes long, unique. Additionally, in 2024 there will be new scenarios for this adventure. Keep in mind that to access, you must measure at least 1.02 m.

Buzz Lightyear Laser Blast: An intergalactic experience! You must help Buzz Lightyear defeat Emperor Zurg by piloting a ship (which rotates 360°) and shooting at the targets on the circuit (marked as Z). It will delight both young and old, and everyone will compete to reach the highest possible score on the individual scoreboards and the overall one, from humble space cadets to the Galactic Hero.

There are some secret tricks to master it and help (or amaze) your children: look for the Zs in the triangles (they score more points) and diamonds, the more hidden or moving, the better; if you hit a good target, shoot several times, you will score even higher. Stay alert, as they can be anywhere, and if you hit Zurg's chest or the red robot's back at the end, you get a super bonus! Good luck!

Autopia by Avis: In this attraction, a classic from Disneyland California in the 1950s, you will drive a retro-futuristic sports car on a rail-guided circuit. Height comes into play here: children who are 1.32 m or taller can drive their own car; and those who measure at least 81 cm can "drive" if accompanied by a co-pilot who is at least 1.32 m tall. If your child is very young, let them hold the wheel while you operate the accelerator. There's no brake, you'll have to use the motor brake and reduce speed.

The duration of the attraction depends on the speed at which you drive the car. If you prefer not to get stuck at the end, go slowly and you'll extend the ride. Since it's outdoors, it closes in bad weather. On sunny days, it's best to wait in line with a refreshing drink. Additionally, drivers receive a driver's licence for this attraction thanks to Avis' sponsorship!

Orbitron: It's a flying carousel where you'll pilot your own spaceship, which you can raise or lower using the built-in control in the cabin. The ride lasts 1 min 30s, and although smooth, it's not recommended for children under 1 year. Tip: ride it at night, it's spectacular when the lights are on!

Les Mystères du Nautilus, a small underground walking tour, where you will come aboard Captain Nemo's famous submarine. It's a bit hidden, to the right of the Orbitron roundabout, by a small lake. It usually has no queue and sometimes becomes a Meet and Greet spot for Donald dressed as a captain.

Walt Disney Studios

The second park of Disneyland Paris, opened in 2002, is dedicated to the world of cinema and Disney's experience on the big screen: the beginnings of Walt Disney in Hollywood, the birth and development of 2D animated films, and the future of 3D and Live-Action animation.

Front Lot

This area at the park's entrance is equivalent to Main Street's beginning. Here you will find the Studio Services (Visitor Assistance Center), the Baby Care Center, the First Aid Point, as well as a large mall with restaurants and shops, the **Studio 1.**

Studio 1 is dedicated to Walt Disney's early days in cinema and decorated like a massive stage with huge sets. It is also a convenient place to have something to eat or grab some snacks before starting to explore the park. If you have time, look for the light control near the "En Coulisse" restaurant, where you can have fun with the kids "controlling Disneyland Paris" by turning various lights on and off in the set.

Another curiosity is that above Studio 1 you can spot a large globe with a Mickey Mouse figure on top. Urban legend says that this Mickey guards a secret and that it is made of copper to serve as a lightning rod during electrical storms in the area.

The expansion and renovation works at Walt Disney Studios will lead to the temporary closure of Studio 1 starting in April 2024, as well as various access restrictions to Toon Studio, Production Courtyard, etc.

Toon Studio:

In this land dedicated to animated cinema, classic and recent Disney films come to life in shows, attractions, and restaurants. The area is starred by **Studio 3 (Animagique Theatre)**, home to the show "Mickey and the Magician", which you will find reviewed in our "Shows" section.

The **Monsters, Inc.** area is small but very well decorated, with Boo's door and scream measuring machines where the beasts can let out all their energy.

Les Tapis Volants (Flying Carpets over Agrabah) is a flying carousel where we will ascend and descend at our will mounted on a magic carpet. The ride lasts for 1 min 30 s. The attraction will be affected by the area's renovation, reopening in October 2024.

Animation Celebration: This mall, located under Mickey's giant hat, is dedicated to animated films. Besides the show "Frozen: A Musical Invitation" and the meeting with Olaf, as you will see in our "Shows" and "Characters" section, you can also enjoy two small secret plans:

- **Animation Academy:** In this animation studio, a "Disney Animator" will teach you to draw a Disney character. The character is chosen randomly by the artist; you won't know which one it is until you are seated at the desk. The workshop lasts about 20 minutes, and you can take the drawing home as a souvenir; also, since the characters change, each time will be a different experience. Sessions take place throughout the day, although the drawing desks are limited and fill up quickly, especially on bad weather days. If your children's (or your own) dream is to be a Disney animator, this is the place!

- Additionally, young animator apprentices cannot miss one of the best-kept secrets in the park, the **Toy Story Zoetrope from Animation Celebration**. It will surprise you!

Worlds of Pixar

In this area, dedicated to the world of Pixar, you will be transported to the films of Disney's most innovative studio through its incredible attractions.

Crush's Coaster: A fun covered roller coaster inspired by the movie Finding Nemo. Riding on the back of a turtle shell, you will experience being caught in an underwater current. It's an exciting and well-themed experience, but don't be fooled by its naive appearance, as the movements are strong, and the spinning car and darkness contribute to a feeling of disorientation.

It's the busiest attraction in the Studios, so you'll need to make use of all the "advantages" listed on this guide to reduce wait times. If you still find long queues, you can connect to the available Wi-Fi to play "Crush Coaster, the game", a free video game created exclusively to play during this queue, where you'll help Crush the turtle surf the Australian current, collecting as many starfishes as possible.

Cars Quatre Roues Rallye: A carousel inspired by the "Smash and Crash Derby" from Cars 3, aboard spinning cars (ride lasts 1 minute 30 seconds). The entrance is themed as Ramon's paint shop, and the sensation that you're about to crash at any moment is very amusing (although not suitable for those prone to motion sickness).

Cars Road Trip: A ride on a train through an American park, surrounded by characters from Cars, with a duration of 7 minutes. It seems designed for very young children as it moves very slowly, but when you reach the canyon area, there is a show featuring water and explosions that will surprise both young and old.

Toy Story Land: In this land, you'll feel as if you've shrunk to the size of Andy's toys! The area is perfectly themed for immersion in the world of Toy Story and has attractions for both adults and children:

-   **RC Racer:** A kind of "pirate ship" that takes you back and forth riding on the remote-controlled car from Toy Story, for 1 minute 30 seconds. Adrenaline lovers, try to sit in the front row, it feels like it's going to fly off the track.

-   **Toy Soldiers Parachute Drop:** A "free fall" attraction themed around toy soldiers and their parachutes. The design and aesthetic is very good, even the safety video is themed, remember not miss the control tower with its guard! The experience lasts 1 minute 30 seconds, and the drops, from a maximum of 27 metres, are not very intense, nothing like the Tower of Terror. The attraction will close for renovation in May.

-   **Slinky Dog Zigzag Spin:** A gentle version of the classic "caterpillar fair ride", this time aboard the Slinky Dog from Toy Story, spinning in circles, going up and down. It lasts approximately 1 minute, which is just right because any longer and the dizziness would be considerable.

Ratatouille Square

Upon entering this area, you'll feel like you're taking a stroll through Paris in the movie, as even the music heard from the terraces adds to the experience. Here you'll find the Ratatouille attraction and the Chez Rémy restaurant, which we review in our Restaurants section.

If throughout the park you find "Hidden Mickeys", the hidden silhouettes of Mickey, in Ratatouille Square, the challenge is to find the "Hidden Rémys"! Like in the movie, the little mice are everywhere, from the sewer covers, mimicking the escape of the colony, to the fountain, and even hidden behind the fences and the tunnel that connects to Toy Story. Some of their silhouettes, like those of the lampposts, are much better seen at night.

These are just a few curiosities, as the entire square is themed after the movie, with the luminous sign of the restaurant, motorcycles and bicycles, personalised street signs, or chef hats on the bollards... don't miss any detail!

Ratatouille Attraction: It's a journey aboard "mouse cars", in 4D (you'll be given glasses when boarding the attraction). It starts calmly, introducing you to Gusteau and Rémy, but when the villainous Chef Skinner discovers you, it becomes a chase through the restaurant. The experience lasts about 5 minutes, it is spectacular (it was one of the biggest investments in this park), and the wait... is usually spectacular too. The Single Rider queue can be your best ally! Essential for both young and old.

Production Courtyard

This land is dedicated to the world of Hollywood and hosts not only the spectacular attraction "Tower of Terror," but also two theatres: Studio Theatre 2 (home to the new show "Together, a Pixar Musical Adventure") and Studio D, home to "Stitch Live!" and "Disney Junior Dream Factory". The area is undergoing a progressive renovation that will turn it into the Theatre District, dedicated to Disney cinemas.

The Twilight Zone Tower of Terror: For adrenaline junkies! It's a roller coaster with various ride configurations (each experience will be different) and different segments of free fall. The effect is enhanced by systems like a cable that pulls the carriage to make you fall faster than gravity would, causing you to fly out of your seat, or the fact that you're secured with a seatbelt rather than an overhead harness like in other intense attractions - buckle up tight!

One of its charms is the story behind the ride. The experience is based on the 1960s science fiction series "The Twilight Zone", and its introduction recreates a fictitious episode with images from the original series.

Legend has it that four hotel guests and the elevator operator disappeared when, during a storm, lightning struck the tower sending them to an unknown dimension. Since then, the hotel has been abandoned, but today the conditions are the same as that stormy night, and this time you will take the journey aboard the service elevator.

Before accessing it, past the changing sign at the entrance, you will pass through several hotel rooms. Don't miss the sign indicating the hotel's floors; the fallen letters hold a mysterious warning… During the dizzying ride, you'll peek through the tower's windows for a few seconds, only to realise... the height from which you're about to drop! Mind the Photo Ride!

Marvel Avenger Campus

This new themed area, inaugurated in 2022, is dedicated to the Marvel Avengers universe. Here, children will feel like they are "part of the team", as the concept is a recruitment centre, and the missions aim to train future superheroes.

Although it currently only has two attractions, this area hosts many encounters with superheroes (summarised in our Characters section) and some outdoor shows, which along with themed restaurants and shops complete the Marvel experience. These are the two attractions of the Campus:

Avengers Assemble: Flight Force: A super-fast roller coaster, where we will travel through space doing loops and spirals on a mission to save Earth alongside Ironman and Captain Marvel. F.R.I.D.A.Y., Tony Stark's artificial intelligence, directs the attraction from a screen at the entrance.

The duration of the ride is just under 1 minute 30 seconds, which is normal considering you'll go from 0 to almost 100 km/h in less than three seconds. Following the normal queue (the Single Rider queue follows a different route), you'll see a state-of-the-art Ironman animatronic.

Pay attention to the trash cans nearby, as one of them is an animatronic that comes to life! Its name is PUSH, and it moves around, talks to visitors, and thanks them for recycling... It's great!

Spiderman W.E.B. Adventures: An interactive family attraction (similar to Buzz Lightyear Laser Blast, but this time equipped with 3D glasses). In it, Peter Parker (portrayed on screen by Tom Holland himself) shows us his latest invention: the Spider-Bots. During the experiment, a virus infects the spider-like bots, causing them to lose control and multiply by the hundreds!

You'll have to help Spiderman stop them by shooting "virtual webs" aboard a vehicle that detects your movements (approximately 3 minutes). As in Buzz Lightyear Laser Blast, each target has an assigned score, and you'll compete to reach the top. In the Marvel shops, they sell "blasters" that, in addition to being toys with effects, allow you to score many more points on the ride... a real treat!

Disney Village

Although the main focus of the **Disney Village** area is on shops, restaurants, and the cinema industry, there's also an "attraction" just in case you're still eager for more! The **PanoraMagique** hot air balloon, located by the lake, rises a few metres above it; a lovely way to see Disneyland Paris from the air. The fee is not included in the park admission and is paid separately, €18 for adults and €12 for children under 12, and the balloon has a capacity for up to 30 people.

Additionally, Disney Village also features cinemas where, of course, the latest Disney releases are screened, in French or with original subtitles.

Shows and Parades

Disneyland Park Shows and Parades

Disney Stars on Parade: The famous Disneyland Park cavalcade takes place every afternoon, starting from the "It's a Small World!" attraction, crossing the central plaza in front of the Castle, and ending at Town Square on Main Street. Don't miss it, it's spectacular, featuring characters of all kinds, princesses, pirates, and even a fire-breathing dragon, all led by Mickey Mouse himself. During festive seasons, the parade is themed, for example, during Halloween, as well as Christmas, St. Patrick's Day, etc.

The start time varies depending on the season, between 5:00 pm and 5:30 pm, so it's advisable to confirm it on the App and arrive early. The parade lasts about 20-25 minutes.

For an extra fee of 19 €, guests can also book at the App a reserved space in front of the Castle, with an unbeatable view of the parade. However, there are also some free good spots to watch them, let's have a look at them!

The first one is near "It's a Small World!", in front of the Bella Notte pizzeria, as this is where the parade starts, and there are even benches to rest while you wait. Once the last float passes by, you can return to the attractions in Fantasyland and Adventureland with much shorter queues, while the rest of the crowd continues waiting for the parade between the Castle and Main Street; keep an eye on the App, it might be the perfect opportunity to ride Peter Pan!

Other key spots to watch it, if you're not in a hurry, are:

- Between **the Castle stage** and **Discoveryland**: along this stretch, until Central Plaza, there are no visitors on both sides of the parade, only on one side, so you'll take better photos (with the Castle in the background instead of the crowd) and the characters will pay more attention to your side since they will only wave on your side.

- From the **central kiosk** on **Main Street** (you'll see the parade with the Castle in the background, and the floats coming directly towards you). Main Street is also a good place to watch the parade if it looks like rain (check our "Travelling in bad weather" section for more covered routes and points).

- Next to **City Hall**, at the entrance of Main Street, although you can't see the Castle and the space is smaller, this makes the characters get much closer to you.

"A Million Splashes of Colours": until September 30th, this show takes up the concept of Disney Dream and Shine Brighter (the 30th-anniversary show), with a small parade full of characters and music, which takes place several times a day (approximately 4 times a day). The characters and dancers will arrive with their float at the plaza in front of the Castle, filling their central stages with dances.

The show will aim to connect two worlds, that of the classic Disney characters (Mickey, Minnie, Donald...) along with more recent additions, such as Asha from Wish or Mirabel from Encanto, in a colourful dance to the rhythm of various Disney and Pixar themes. The best place to see it is in the center of the stages, you'll be surrounded by music!

The Lion King: The Rhythms of the Earth: In this show, which takes place at the Frontierland Theatre, 30 singers and dancers perform live the soundtrack of the movie, dressed in 400 spectacular costumes, in this 30-minute show. With the release of the movie "Mufasa" on July 5, 2024, special events are expected around this show, and the Hakuna Matata restaurant.

The show is very popular, so it's advisable to arrive well in advance. Disney also offers two ways to shorten the wait and ensure a seat. The first option is to book seats through the park's website or app, at an extra fee of €15 per person.

The second guaranteed access option was only for MasterCard cardholders, as, till April 2024, it offered free priority tickets (the number was very limited, between 25 and 30 tickets per show).

If the offer gets back, just go to City Hall on Main Street at least two hours before the time you want to attend the show (better 2 hours and 15 minutes). At City Hall, you'll see two queues, choose the one on the right, and just two hours before the show starts, a Cast Member will distribute up to 5 priority access tickets for each MasterCard you show. Sometimes they also ask for ID to confirm the identity of the cardholder.

Once you have the priority tickets, head to the theatre 30 minutes before the show starts. The MasterCard seats were quite close to the stage, and centred. When the show is over, you can even go to Studio Services for new priority tickets for another show that has them available.

Mickey's PhilharMagic: At the Discoveryland Theatre, Mickey's best friend, Donald Duck, has prepared this 4D show that will take you through Disney's most unforgettable soundtracks. The show lasts just under 15 minutes and is usually not overly crowded.

Disney Performing Arts On-Stage: Videopolis and Main Street host this amateur music, dance, and theatre festival where hundreds of youth and amateur groups participate each year, coming from all over the world.

Night time Shows at Disneyland Park:

Disney Dreams!: The night time spectacle takes place every evening as the "grand finale" of the park and turns Sleeping Beauty Castle into a giant screen with music, projections, and incredible special effects involving water and fire. The show lasts approximately 25 minutes and concludes with an impressive fireworks display. It's worth planning an evening to see it; you can't miss it!

The show revisits beloved classics with the help of Tinker Bell and shines even brighter as many attendees purchase Disney Light'Ears, earpieces equipped with technology that changes colour to the rhythm of Disney Dreams music.

The best views of the show are in the centre of the square in front of the Castle or behind the square's stages, as you'll avoid many phones and children sitting on shoulders. However, these spots are highly coveted and require waiting well in advance. Another less known location with a clear view of the Castle is at the entrance of Discoveryland along the railing without stepping on the grass.

If the weather is good, it's best to grab takeaway dinner (for example, at Café Hyperion) and enjoy it while you wait. If you don't want to spend too much time waiting, another option is to watch the show from the sides of the Castle (for example, near the entrance to Adventureland).

Once the fireworks are over, the crowd leaves the park heading to the station. If you need to leave early or don't want to be surrounded by the crowd, it's best to watch from Main Street. You won't be as close to the show, but you'll be in a prime position for the exit.

As for the parade, there are exclusive spaces in front of the castle that can be booked through the park's App for an extra fee of €19.

On the night of **July, the 14th**, to celebrate France's National Day, an additional fireworks show takes place over the Castle, paying tribute to the host country, right after Disney Dreams!

This day will feature classics from Disney and Pixar set in France, such as Ratatouille, The Aristocats, Beauty and the Beast, or The Hunchback of Notre-Dame, with a combination of drones, pyrotechnics, projections on the Castle, and music, not forgetting French symbols, from the Eiffel Tower to the tricolour flag or the rosette of Notre-Dame de Paris.

There is also a Christmas version, **Disney Dreams! of Christmas,** which is projected from November to January, with Olaf as host guiding through many more wintry scenes from Frozen, 101 Dalmatians...

As previously mentioned, amongst the novelties of 2024, and until September 30th, a new pre-show of about 10 minutes will take place before the fireworks show. Under the name "**Disney Electrical Sky Parade**", it will fill the sky over the Castle with a myriad of "illuminated floats" with up to 500 drones.

This show pays homage to various elements of the original Disneyland Paris night time parade, **"Main Street Electrical Parade",** which took place from 1992 to 2003, such as Mickey's train or Cinderella's Carriage. It's an opportunity for many visitors to return to their childhood, this time accompanied by their children.

Shows at Walt Disney Studios.

Mickey and the Magician: This magical musical spectacle takes place at the Animagique Theatre (Toon Studio), and is full of tricks, special effects, and cameos from other Disney characters. Perhaps it should be called "Mickey and the Magicians" since this apprentice will have to master the tricks of Disney's most powerful sorcerers: the Fairy Godmother, Rafiki, Aladdin's Genie... The show lasts 25 minutes, and is the most popular in the park. As such, the queue tends to be very significant.

Tickets for guaranteed access can be purchased through the app at a price of €15 per person. Until recently, MasterCard also offered priority tickets for this show, obtained at Studio Services similar to those for The Lion King at City Hall, don't hesitate to check with them.

Frozen: A Musical Invitation: Travel to Arendelle's Kingdom in this interactive musical show at Animation Celebration Theatre (right under Mickey's huge hat, in Toon Studio), The dialogues and songs mix English and French, but are quite easy to follow, even for young fans.

The show, about 25 minutes long, takes place in several stages, where you'll sing with Anna, Kristoff, and Sven while preparing a final surprise for Elsa. Even Olaf is ready to give "warm hugs"! The show is very popular, with only 200 seats, giving a fairly close feeling to the characters; remember to arrive early so you don't miss out.

Disney Junior Dream Factory: In this 20-minute show at Studio D in the Production Courtyard, Mickey and Minnie perform and dance accompanied by Disney Junior characters! like Vampirina, to operate Disney's dream machine, while smoke bubbles fall from the ceiling, impressive!

For this show, MasterCard also offers fast access tickets to its cardholders. In this case, you also have to go at least two hours before the showtime (2 hours 15 minutes is even better) to Studio Services, where you will receive up to five priority access tickets for each MasterCard you show.

With them, simply go to the entrance of Studio D thirty minutes before the show starts, and you'll have seats centred and close to the stage.

Stitch Live!: An interactive show at Studio D (Production Courtyard) where you'll chat with Disney's most lovable alien on a giant screen. Several magic tricks make Stitch interact in real-time with the audience. Although there are seats, children are encouraged to sit in front so Stitch can see them better. At first, it may seem a bit static, but he will soon choose a child—or adult!—to talk to.

The theatre can host 200 spectators and it usually fills up quickly, but in return, the experience is more intimate. Additionally, since Stitch interacts differently each time, no two shows are the same.

The show lasts 15-20 minutes, and it's a popular choice if there's bad weather and some outdoor attractions are closed, as the theatre has a sheltered queue area, where you can enjoy different projections and a pre-show. Languages are English and French, and the schedules vary, check the most up-to-date one on the app. With the release of Lilo and Stitch's Live-Action movie, on May 10, 2024, special encounters and news are expected around this attraction.

Together: A Pixar Musical Adventure: Premiered in the summer of 2023, the new show at the Studio Theatre is an immersive spectacle with live music, telling an original and emotional story through scenes from Pixar's most famous movies, from Toy Story to Monsters, Inc. The duration of the show is about 30 minutes, and you can purchase guaranteed access tickets through the app at a price of €15 per person.

"Alice & the Queen of Hearts: Back to Wonderland": In spring 2024, a ground-breaking musical show about the world of Alice in Wonderland will arrive at the park, bringing together artists from different disciplines, in a show with two alternative endings that will be decided by the audience! The show will take place near the Avengers Campus, at the Stunt Show Arena, which was home, until the pandemic, to the "Moteurs... Action!" stunt show.

Shows at Marvel Avengers Campus:

Heroic Welcome: The Avengers make an appearance alongside the Quinjet, their plane, at the entrance of the Avengers Campus. This show takes place several times a day; check the schedule on the app to try to coincide your arrival at the Avengers Campus with their greeting—it'll be the best welcome!

The Amazing Spider-Man: Everyone's favourite superhero performs a stunt show on the rooftop of his attraction, Spider-Man W.E.B. Adventure. Check the schedule on the app as there are performances per day, and you can't afford to miss it. It's perfect for entertaining yourself while awaiting your appointment at the Hero Training Center (the character meeting point) or if you are enjoying a snack at the Campus food trucks.

Avengers Unite!: Black Widow and Black Panther engage in an epic battle against Taskmaster on the rooftop of Spider-Man W.E.B. Adventure. It's a spectacle of acrobatics and combat with several shows daily. Check the schedule on the app; it'll leave your little ones in awe.

Guardians of the Galaxy: Dance Challenge!: Join Gamora, Star-Lord, and Mantis in a fun dance choreography near the Avengers Assemble: Flight Force attraction. This "flash-mob" has multiple daily performances; don't hesitate to check the schedule on the App.

Warriors of Wakanda: Black Panther's allies, the Warriors of Wakanda, led by General Okoye, will put on a fighting display in front of Avengers Assemble: Flight Force. The show takes place several times a day, and they even select several "recruits" to participate in the exhibition and try their weapons—don't miss out!

At the end of 2024, **Marvel Avengers Campus** will be the stage for a brand-new night time activation, which will come to life every evening on the Worldwide Engineering Brigade building (close to Spiderman attraction), until Spring 2025. This engaging experience will combine projections, music and special effects with an all-new storyline, featuring some favourite and new-to-Disneyland Paris Marvel characters. Although details haven't been disclosed, it's most likely to resemble two of the most successful night shows at Walt Disney Studios: Avengers: Power the Night and Magic Over Disney.

Avengers: Power the Night: Although currently unavailable, we can't help but mention this night time show with drones and projections expected to return soon to Disneyland Paris, following the two seasons of 2023. Spectacular projections of Marvel heroes, fireworks, sound, special effects, and 500 drones in a unique show over the Tower of Terror in Production Courtyard—the perfect ending to your visit!

Magic Over Disney: Similarly, the return of the light show to the Studios' night is expected soon. The Tower of Terror becomes the stage for this show that covers Disney's great classics, Pixar's most unforgettable movies, and the best soundtracks.

Recommended Itineraries

Plan your day in advance, taking into account everyone's preferences, the weather, and the crowd. To help you, we've prepared several general tips for planning your route and some sample itineraries; although there are as many possible routes as families visiting Disneyland Paris.

The first recommendation is to arrive early, not only to take advantage of Extra Magic Time (if you're staying at a Disney hotel) or Rope Dropping, but also because wait times for attractions will increase minute by minute. By noon, queues reach their peak, and you'll have to wait in long lines. If you arrive at the parks right at opening, you can enjoy the attractions with waits of less than 5 minutes.

Download the App, monitor wait times, and confirm the closing schedule for attractions. If you see a highly sought-after attraction (Peter Pan, Big Thunder Mountain..) with a 10-15 minute wait at any point, go directly and as quickly as possible because many visitors will see it at the same time and set off, so in less than five minutes, that queue can become much larger.

Also, consider Single Rider lines and Baby Switch options, as well as Disney Premier Access passes to save time in lines.

One-Day Itinerary at Disneyland Park

If you're visiting the park for just one day, it's best to focus on Disneyland Park, its attractions, and outdoor shows, especially if your kids are small. It's more themed around the Disney universe (at least until the new areas open in 2024 and 2025) and boasts attractions for the whole family. Focus on the park's most special attractions and outdoor parades and shows. Some passages from our "Covered Walkways" section will help you get from one point to another, and if your budget allows, it's a good idea to buy "Disney Premier Access" to ride as many attractions as possible.

Start your day as early as possible, during Extra Magic Time if you're staying at a Disney hotel. In those first minutes with low attendance, the key is to enjoy one of the two busiest attractions: Peter Pan's Flight or Big Thunder Mountain, depending on whether your kids age and their appetite for more intense thrills.

Arriving in Fantasyland through the Castle early in the day is one of the most "magical" ways to start your visit to Disneyland Paris. Head through Main Street to Sleeping Beauty Castle, walk through it to reach Peter Pan's Flight, which will be your first attraction. Once in Fantasyland, there are many attractions you can visit, such as the Teacups, Snow White, or the Labyrinth, some of them suitable for babies or pregnant women. If the queue is short, you can meet Mickey at his Meet Mickey dressing room, but avoid the Princess Pavilion; the wait there would consume your entire morning.

Just before noon, when attractions have the longest queues, you can explore Adventureland, with several queues-free rides like Skull Rock, Adventure Island, and the Robinsons' Treehouse. You can also look for characters, ride Pirates of the Caribbean or Indiana Jones, and grab a quick snack to delay lunchtime (use Mobile Order Pickup at Hakuna Matata restaurant, or grab something quick at the kiosks).

During lunchtime, the crowds at attractions decrease, making it a perfect time to ride Big Thunder Mountain and discover Phantom Manor and Boot Hill Cemetery if your kids are older, otherwise, take them to the Lion King show in Frontierland. Then, you can have a late lunch at one of the quick-service restaurants in the area, such as Cowboy Cookout Barbecue.

Before 17:00, make sure to be by the "It's a Small World!" attraction. The afternoon parade starts from there, and while most visitors go to see it in front of the Castle or on Main Street, you can watch the parade here and then go enjoy the attractions you missed in Fantasyland with very little queue. It could be a good time to ride Peter Pan if you missed it, or enjoy the Teacups with the lamps lit at sunset. Next, complete your visit by touring Discoveryland. Towards the end of the afternoon, many visitors start leaving the park to catch flights or head home, and the queues for high-traffic attractions like Buzz Lightyear Laser Blast or Hyperspace Mountain decrease.

If you haven't had the chance to ride BTM, do it from 20:00 onwards, but don't miss it. Try to delay dinner time as well (a good option is to pre-order with Mobile Food Order), or grab a take away to enjoy while waiting for the night time show

Two-Day Itinerary at Disneyland Park:

In a two-day itinerary focused on Disneyland Park, in addition to riding almost all the attractions, you can book a table-service restaurant or character dining experience or watch indoor shows like The Lion King. If your kids are older and looking for more thrilling rides, you can visit Disneyland Park on the first day and dedicate the second day to Walt Disney Studios.

If you spend both days at Disneyland Park, our recommendation is to start the day early, using Extra Magic Time if possible, or booking the first character breakfast if you're staying at a Disney hotel. Go through the Castle (either through its interior or via the Dragon's Lair) to Fantasyland—don't miss that arrival at the Park, it's the most classic! Head first to the Peter Pan attraction (where the queue will increase by the minute), and continue exploring this Land and its other attractions. Queue times will peak around 12:30 p.m. a good time to enjoy attractions with shorter waiting times (like Alice's Curious Labyrinth); explore Fantasyland and Adventureland in search of characters, or grab a quick snack to delay lunchtime.

During lunchtime, from 1 to 2 p.m., attraction queues will drop again, giving you a chance, if you're lucky, to enjoy high-traffic attractions like Big Thunder Mountain. Have lunch as late as possible, but if you're aiming for a slightly less rushed visit, you can book a table-service restaurant that provides an experience, such as Captain Jack's, the Pirate's Restaurant, or The Lucky Nugget Saloon in Frontierland.

A little before 5, it's advisable to be near the It's a Small World! attraction to watch the afternoon parade. When the last float passes by, you'll have another great opportunity to ride Fantasyland attractions with short queues while most people are watching the parade between the Castle and Main Street. Fantasyland closes an hour before the park's closing time to prepare for the fireworks, so it's best not to leave it until late afternoon.

Upon returning to the hotel, recharge both your own batteries and those of your phones and cameras, and review the plan for the next day. Don't forget to check in for your flights if check-in is already open. If you're staying at a Disney hotel, your little ones will probably remind you that Mickey will wake them up tomorrow (don't forget to program it by phone using the Wake-up button).

On the second day, use the EMT or the early hours of the day to ride Big Thunder Mountain, if you didn't get to it the first day (although you can also try during the night time show; the experience is spectacular). Enjoy discovering corners of the park and meeting characters.

Since you already saw the parade the day before (unless the little fans want to repeat), use the afternoon to explore Discoveryland with fewer queues, starting with Buzz Lightyear Laser Blast. If you want to move quickly around the park to ride attractions again, use the routes from our "Covered Walkways". They're perfect for moving around in bad weather and getting quickly from one point to another.

One-Day Itinerary at Walt Disney Studios:

If you have slightly older children who love thrilling rides, or if you're spending more than two days at Disneyland Paris, you can't miss Walt Disney Studios.

Start the day as early as possible, preferably during Extra Magic Time, at one of the "top" attractions: Crush's Coaster or Spider-Man W.E.B. Adventures (plus, you'll be able to see the Avengers' Heroic Welcome at the entrance of the Avengers Campus). Next, adrenaline enthusiasts can't miss The Tower of Terror, and both children and adults will enjoy Mickey and the Magician; Pixar: Together, Frozen: A Musical Invitation, or the new Alice in Wonderland show.

For lunch, consider returning to the Avengers Campus and booking at the fun PYM buffet. Alternatively, grab something from one of the food trucks, which are economical and varied, while watching superhero shows or waiting for your turn at the meet-and-greet at the Hero Training Centre.

In the afternoon, explore the Toy Story area, ending at sunset in the Ratatouille section as its Parisian square lights up. The Ratatouille attraction is usually very crowded, so make sure to prioritise it on your agenda and adjust your plan accordingly so you don't miss it. For dinner, you can snack at the stalls of the Rendez-Vous Gourmet market or book dinner at Chez Rémy. Although the price is higher, and being a table-service restaurant takes a little longer, the decoration is spectacular, and the experience is worth it.

As night falls, Walt Disney Studios closes a little earlier than Disneyland Park, so if there's no show scheduled at the Studios on that day, you might have time for one last stroll through the park, repeat some attractions (except those in Fantasyland, which will be closed), or watch the fireworks over the Castle.

Divide and Conquer: Combining Attractions

If you're travelling with children of very different ages, the youngest may not be able to ride some attractions with the older ones, due to age or height restrictions. In those moments, if you're two adults, it's best to use the Single Rider queue or the Baby Switch so that the other adult can ride later. For safety reasons, children under 7 years old must be accompanied by an adult on all attractions. In the following table, we show you alternative plans to combine in these cases and keep everyone entertained.

Attractions for Babies and Toddlers		
Attraction	**Restrictions / Recommendations**	**Alternatives**
Disneyland Park		
Dumbo the Flying Elephant	Not recommended for children under 1 year of age	Le Pays des Contes de Fées
Le Train du Cirque	Not suitable for children under 1 year of age	Le Pays des Contes de Fées
Indiana Joneas and the Temple of Peril	Minimum height 1.40 m.	La Cabane des Robinsons
Pirates of the Caribbean	May frighten younger guests	Adventure Island / Aladdin's Enchanted Passage
Big Thunder Mountain	Minimum height 1.02 m.	Frontierland Playground / The Lion King
Phantom Manor	May frighten younger guests	The Lion King / Thunder Mesa Riverboat Landing
Hyperspace Mountain	Minimum height 1.20 m.	Buzz Lightyear Laser Blast
Star Tours	Minimum height 1.02 m.	Star Port Encounter
Orbitron	Not recommended for children under 1 year of age	Buzz Lightyear Laser Blast
Autopia	Minimum height 0.81 m.	Mickey's Phillarmagic
Walt Disney Studios		
RC Racer	Minimum height 1.20 m.	Slinky Dog Zig Zag Spin
Toy Soldiers Parachute Drop	Minimum height 0.81 m.	Cars Quatre Roues Rallye
The Tower of Terror	Minimum height 1.02 m.	Stitch Live!
Crush's Coaster	Minimum height 1.07 m.	Les Tapis Volants

Queue Entertainment

Disneyland is a dream place... for everyone! Therefore, queues at attractions and waits for parades are quite common. Part of the attraction queues were designed with this in mind and are also themed, such as in Star Tours, Ratatouille, or Pirates of the Caribbean, to immerse you in the attraction from the beginning. In addition to this, there are airplane or subway rides and waits at restaurants, so it's best to arm yourself with patience... and tricks!

To keep your little ones entertained during the wait, after you've exhausted classics like **"I Spy"**, **"Rock, Paper, Scissors"** (extend it with some "Friends" elements such as Fire and Water Balloon), or **Nonsense**, why not try the **"20 Questions"**- Disney version? Bring stickers, each participant puts a sticker on the forehead of the person next to them, with a Disney character written on it, and that person has to guess who their character is in 20 questions with "yes or no" answers from the others—or try to guess which character they're thinking of! There are countless variations! Think of games that are easy to stop and start without any hassle, and ensure they're easy and fun so all children can participate in them.

Another suitable option in the park is the **"Disney Movie Game"**—you'll have a blast guessing or acting out! Try also the ABCs of Countries: going through the alphabet, each player must say a country or city starting with that letter, taking turns. Whoever can't think of another option is eliminated, and you move on to the next letter. Will you make it to Z?

You can also bring along **pocket-sized surprises** to help pass the time. Stores like "Flying Tiger" offer many portable items like colouring or scratch books, puzzles, card games, "Where's Waldo?" books, notebooks that you can use for collaborative drawing, playing STOP, or writing a story... Any of these can fit into your backpack, ready to be pulled out when needed.

Kids love **face painting**, especially **glow-in-the-dark** paints, a perfect resource, for example, during the Buzz Lightyear queue to ride the attraction with painted faces, or during the wait before the night time parade. You may even add glowing sticks or bracelets! Another idea is to print out a **park map** for each child—they'll learn to navigate and you can decide in line which attraction to visit next.

For budding artists, a great option is the **"Mystères Disney Trompe l'oeil"** colouring books, where they only discover the character as they colour it. Another fun activity to do with them is to play **"This is not"**: start drawing with something obvious, like a cloud, and challenge your kids to turn it into anything... but a cloud!

For younger children, "water marker" colouring books are very practical, never running out and easily exchangeable amongst them. Bubble blowers (place them with the other liquids in your luggage if you travel by plane) or, as a last resort, a Mickey helium balloon tied to the stroller will not fail.

Surely you've already noticed, but there are **Hidden Mickeys** all over the park. Maybe it's just his silhouette, ears or some outfit detail. Sometimes you may need to play with perspective to align the circles, but they are everywhere!

At the end of the guide, there's a checklist with some of them— the first to spot a Hidden Mickey wins and can write their initials on the list. At the end of the day, count them up and see who located the most Mickeys from the list. It will keep the kids with their eyes wide open all over the park! Hidden Mickeys started as an "internal joke" by the Imagineers, although they now inhabit every corner of the park. Disney has never confirmed their existence or published a complete list, so you may discover some that no one else has seen!

If you find yourself needing to allow your children some screen time, bring along a game that can be played offline, as several indoor queues have no mobile coverage.

Lastly, a child that is bored in a queue is always, always hungry. Don't forget the **snacks**—bringing snacks and lunches will save many waiting moments (and your budget). In our "Backpack" section, you'll find many snack ideas ideal for kids.

Characters

A magical aspect of the Disney experience is meeting the characters. From the authentic Mickey and his friends, to the princesses, Marvel superheroes, or Star Wars characters, everyone has a favourite that will make them excited.

After the pandemic, close interactions with characters have returned; your kids will be able to approach and hug them, take photos (it's not mandatory to buy the official ones from the photographers), and also ask for autographs. Bring along a notebook for this purpose (in the park there are very special editions, with specific sections for photos, but they come at a premium), preferably with a hard cover to support when signing, and a thick pen or marker that is easy to grab by the characters' huge and soft hands.

You can also get creative: for example, some visitors take photos with an **instant camera** and the character signs it, or use a **picture frame mat** to frame their favourite photo from the trip afterward. Another good idea is to bring a book of Disney characters like the **"Disney Who's Who Encyclopedia",** with over 150 entries, where each character can sign their corresponding photo.

To avoid crowds, characters are normally found at planned **"Meet and Greet" points** or at restaurants hosting meet up events (as described in the Restaurants sections).

"Meet and Greet" locations are announced in the App (marked with a Mickey head), but there are also surprise "Meet and Greet" spots (watch out for green and beige tents or umbrellas, and the characters you come across).

In general, it's easier to see characters in the morning, between 10 a.m. and 1 p.m., as in the afternoon many take part in the parades, and, naturally, they don't duplicate. To make it easy to meet your favourite characters, check out the following hiding spots.

Mickey Mouse

As we know that Mickey is the most sought-after character by both young and old, courtesy of the personal secretary of the "Boss" himself, we've managed to obtain Mickey's schedule!

- Early in the morning, during Extra Magic Time, you can find him welcoming visitors alongside Minnie from the balcony of **Main Street Station.**

- Between 10 a.m., and 5 p.m., you'll find him at the **"Meet Mickey Mouse"** theatre in Fantasyland, located under the train stop, very close to the Peter Pan attraction. As the most popular character, the queue often exceeds 60 minutes. Fortunately, the venue it's indoors and Mickey short films are shown on a giant screen to entertain the wait. You'll see Mickey in his dressing room for a few minutes and have the opportunity to take photos with him.

  Pay attention to the dressing room, as there are many nods to various movies (Mary Poppins, Dumbo, Fantasia, The Aristocats...). His costume and gloves are ready for his next performance, as Mickey never misses the afternoon parade between Fantasyland and Main Street, and usually rides on the first float. After the parade, around 5:30 p.m., he returns to the dressing room until 7 p.m. (check the App).

- Throughout the day, he usually has several **Meet and Greet encounters** in the park, whose schedules are announced in the App. Generally, they take place at two points in Frontierland: in front of the Phantom Manor haunted mansion and at the Cowboy Cookout restaurant, where he'll be "dressed for the occasion".

- Mickey and Minnie are two lovebirds, so Minnie usually visits Mickey at these points, and Mickey visits her at the Meet and Greet in Discoveryland (named "Around the World") or at Walt Disney Studios park, in the Front Lot.

- Also in the Studios, Mickey offers an essential show, called **Mickey and the Magician,** at the Animagique Theatre. It's very popular, so it's best to reserve access through the App and arrive 30 minutes before the show starts.

- Another show Mickey participates in is **Disney Junior Dream Factory,** which returns on May 26, 2023, to Studio D in the Production Courtyard, at the Studios. In this musical show, you'll join Mickey, Minnie, and their Disney Junior friends to repair the "dream machine" through different songs.

- In the late afternoon, he often goes with his friends to the Meet and Greet points at **Disney hotels** Newport Bay Club, Sequoia Lodge, and Santa Fe, generally dressed "for the occasion", according to the theme of the hotel. Confirm with the hotel reception the schedule for these Meet and Greet sessions and try to find out which character will be there.

- At night, in Disneyland Park, he usually dines at the **Plaza Gardens restaurant** on Main Street, a buffet restaurant with character encounters, accompanied by his friends (you'll find all the details in our Restaurants section).

- Lastly, at the end of the day, Mickey bids farewell to visitors from the top of Main Street Station, in what's called "**Mickey's Goodnight Kiss**", where he greets and says a few words. It usually starts about 10 minutes after the Disney Dreams fireworks end, and repeats every 10-15 minutes until closing.

Disney Princesses

This chapter is going to be a bit extensive, but "noblesse oblige". If you have little fans of Disney royalty, here are all the tricks to know where to find them, starting with the two most obvious places, the Auberge and the Pavilion, but also the "secret" hideouts of their royal highnesses, to see them with fewer queues and no extra cost.

- **Cinderella's Auberge in Fantasyland**. In this table-service restaurant you enjoy lunch or dinner in the company of Disney princesses. Princess breakfasts are currently exclusive to the Castle Club Lounge at the Disneyland Hotel. It's essential to reserve at the Auberge, and in the "Restaurants" section, you'll find price and menu information.

The princesses usually found at the Auberge are Cinderella, as this is her restaurant, and Aurora, since she's the owner of the Castle. They're accompanied by Cinderella's two mice, and another two princesses such as Snow White, Belle, Ariel, Rapunzel, or Merida. Other less common visitors may be Tiana, Mulan, Jasmine, Pocahontas, and Moana (who usually attend meetings in the lands), and the princes. Sometimes Minnie also joins the cast dressed as a princess.

- **Princess Pavilion in Fantasyland**. Perhaps the most challenging experience to enjoy, as it has the longest queue times in the entire park (even longer than what the signs announce). We recommend trying only if your little one is hardcore fan of Disney royalty and meeting them is their "must-have experience" of the entire park.

Wait times range from 1 hour to the record of 4 hours to spend 5 minutes with the princess, who speaks English or French, and take some photos. Once you reach the meeting point, a Cast Member will tell you which princess you will be meeting (you can't choose, although they usually make exceptions if it coincides with the costume your children are wearing).

The pavilion opens at 8:30 a.m., making it ideal to take advantage of the EMH and head straight there very quickly, you'll avoid lengthy queues. Don't be misled if you see a few people outside (where a sign indicates which princesses are present on that day), the line continues inside, in a corridor decorated with elements of the characters (Cinderella's shoe, Snow White's apple, etc.).

The wait only decreases slightly during the evening parade, between 5 and 6 p.m.. The place typically closes at 7 p.m., although it's advisable to check the times on the App.

Don't despair if you don't have the chance to visit the Pavilion or the Auberge; there are many options to meet some of your favourite princesses. These include the **Kids Club** or the **Castle Lounge** of the **Disneyland Hotel**, as well as in the **parades**, just to name a few. However, there are many more ways!

While the most "classic and delicate" princesses are often indoors and harder to see, there are others eager to explore their "territories" (settings that match the character), like Jasmine and Aladdin near Agrabah Café, Moana and Mulan in Adventureland, Merida in the forested area of Frontierland, or Rapunzel in Fantasyland. Speaking of Disney's most famous mane, pay attention, if you find Flynn Rider, ask him what he's carrying in the saddlebag; he might surprise you by showing you Rapunzel's crown!

In general, princesses tend to be more present during the summer, while animated characters, who dress in a more suitable manner for cold weather, are more likely to be seen in winter. The schedules for **Meet and Greet** sessions are in the App's program, and surprise Meet and Greets usually take place in the morning, between 11 a.m., and lunchtime.

Right after that, the "classic" princesses typically go to the Pavilion and the Auberge, perhaps you'll run into them on the way (since every so often the princesses go to rest as they rotate). In the afternoon, you can see princesses and characters returning from their encounters between Pizzeria Bella Notte and It's a Small World!, to take part in the parade that starts from that spot. A handy tip is to pass through the Castle and turn right. Beyond the Auberge, past Cinderella's carriage, there's a fence and a door through which the princesses go on their way to their meals; they won't stop, but you'll be able to see them, wave from afar, and sometimes shake hands.

Additionally, the park sometimes schedules special events with a greater presence of Princesses, such as the Princess and Pirates Festival or the Grand Princess Party. For 2024, special events celebrating the releases of new movies like the Snow White Live-Action and Moana 2, or events related to Rapunzel's new attraction are expected.

- **Elsa and Anna from Frozen:** Although the sisters from Arendelle used to appear together in the Pavilion, this combination often resulted in even longer queues. Right now, visitors can see the Norwegian princesses sing and dance in the "Frozen: A Musical Invitation" show, at the Animation Celebration theatre.

  Olaf, Elsa's snowman, has a Meet and Greet spot in the Studios, in the Animation Academy area, next to the Animation Celebration theatre. It's advisable to visit it just during the "Frozen: A Musical Invitation" show, as it usually gets crowded afterwards. The queue for Olaf, like for Minnie Mouse, closes a little earlier than the Meet and Greet time, so it's better to plan ahead if you don't want to miss out. Also, with the opening of the new Frozen-themed area, scheduled for 2024, more attractions and encounters around Arendelle are expected.

During special themed seasons you will encounter exclusive characters, such as Santa Claus, Santa Stitch, and Santa Goofy during the Christmas season; or villains like Maleficent, Jack Skellington, Cruella, or Jafar, who take over the park at Halloween.

Although these are the main favourites, there are many more that you'll come across at different Meet and Greet points (keep an eye on the green or beige umbrellas) and surprise encounters, always in places most related to their story.

Encounters in Disneyland Park

- In **Main Street,** you'll typically encounter many of Mickey's friends (especially during the EMT), Uncle Scrooge, Thumper, or Winnie the Pooh characters, along with Stitch and Max. Mary Poppins and Marie from The Aristocats, the most elegant, are usually found near the central plaza kiosk.

- In **Fantasyland**, it's common to encounter characters from Alice in Wonderland near the maze, such as the Mad Hatter, the Queen of Hearts, or Alice herself, but also Cinderella's stepsisters Anastasia and Drizella.

- Woody and Jessie, the Toy Story cowboys, often stroll through **Frontierland**, as does Jack Skellington; the latter, around Phantom Manor.

- In **Adventureland**, characters such as Peter Pan, Captain Hook, or Mr. Smee are located in the Pirates area (Jack Sparrow also usually makes an appearance in the evening). Near the restaurants in this land, you can usually find characters from The Lion King (near Hakuna Matata Restaurant), The Jungle Book (at Colonel Hathi's Pizza Outpost) or Chip and Dale dressed as explorers...

- In **Discoveryland**, unlike other lands, there is a smaller presence of characters, with the exception of the Star Port (under the X-Wing ship), where you can find Darth Vader, and a meeting point with the Mandalorian (who carries Baby Yoda in his bag) has recently been added. During special festivities, such as May the 4th (the famous "Star Wars Day" or "May the Force"), there are Stormtrooper parades, and characters like Chewbacca, R2-D2, Rey, or Kylo-Ren join the encounters.

Encounters in Walt Disney Studios

With the upcoming expansion of the Studios, which will include a new **Frozen** area, a **Tangled** attraction, and most likely a new land dedicated to **The Lion King** or **Star Wars**, more meeting points, experiences and activities involving characters are to be expected. Dates and details haven't been confirmed yet.

Currently, Goofy and Buzz Lightyear have their own meeting points at the entrance, as do Rémy and Linguini in the Ratatouille square. Mike Wazowski and Sully, as well as the Toy Story characters, also have their own meeting points on their respective lands. Additionally, fans of Lightning McQueen can see him driving around the Production Courtyard area, in an impromptu "mini parade".

Until recently, character encounters at Walt Disney Studios had to be booked through the Lineberty app. Currently, the park's own app offers a system to make reservations, valid for the Hero Training Centre in the Avengers Campus.

Superheroes

- The **Hero Training Centre** serves as a meeting point for superheroes. It operates with a virtual queue system, where you can join the line for one specific member of the Avengers, or choose the surprise encounter. The regular superheroes are Spider-Man, Iron-Man, and Captain Marvel, while any Marvel hero may show up for surprise encounters.

  This queue can be accessed via the park's App, under the map section "Characters > Walt Disney Studios > Hero Training Centre", and grants access after linking your ticket or reservation in the app.

  Virtual queue slots are free and available twice a day, at 10 a.m. and 2:15 p.m. Remember to set an alarm so you don't miss out. You can reserve one encounter per day, and you must be inside the park at that moment (all participants in the encounter must have entered the park).

  Once your reservation countdown is over you can access the Hero Training Centre where, after a short wait, you'll meet the superhero. During this encounter, you can take photos and videos, and Disney's own photographers take photos and videos with effects; if you want to purchase them, you can find all the details in our "Photopass" section.

- If you don't get a slot at the Hero Training Centre, don't worry, there are other options to see superheroes. In our "Shows" section, all their parades, heroic greetings, and rooftop appearances are listed. Additionally, just like in Disneyland Park, superheroes come and go from their shows and encounters.

  For example, you can grab something from the food trucks at the Marvel Avengers Campus in the afternoon and sit at the tables in front of the Super Diner, where you might see Marvel superheroes on their way to the encounters and shows they participate in.

  Additionally, guests at the Hotel New York - The Art of Marvel can book an encounter with superheroes at the Super Hero Station, through the App.

Why is it sometimes difficult to see Disney characters? In theory, part of the experience is that characters are not available at all times, and for children, it's magical to encounter their favourites. Additionally, their appearances are carefully planned to maintain that magical effect, ensuring that characters are never "duplicated" meaning that two "Mickeys" are never seen at the same time.

Did you know...? The Disney character casting and auditions are quite rigorous; not only do applicants have to have specific height requirements for each character, but also communication and dance skills. Only the best candidates get the lead character roles (Mickey, Minnie) and "face characters" of princesses and villains.

Characters receive lessons to connect with visitors, which includes learning the character's signature - always the same in any Disney park where they are - or their expressions and way of speaking.

The most "human" characters (princesses or pirates) usually speak English and French, and sometimes a third language. Encourage children to ask them about their story; there's nothing better than hearing something from the protagonist's tale.

"Non-human" characters communicate through gestures, and if you mention their hobbies or skills, they'll represent them. In any case, if your children (like many of them) are shy, a fun activity is to discuss with them questions in advance so that it feels natural, "what would you ask this character if you saw them?".

Restaurants in Disneyland París

Throughout Disneyland Paris, including both parks, the Village area, and the hotels, visitors can choose from a wide range of restaurants and cafes offering a variety of food and ambiance, grouped into four different categories.

-   **Table service restaurants:** require reservation in advance, which you can make up to two months prior to your visit, or even earlier for many of them if you are staying at a Disney hotel. In this case, make your reservation as soon as you receive the confirmation of your hotel reservation.

    A Cast Member will accompany you to your table, and you can order dishes from the fixed menu included in your Meal Plans, or choose from the à la carte menu. Prices are higher, but it is also a more enjoyable experience, with better dishes and an elaborate ambiance. If you are short on time, keep in mind that this is the slowest option, with longer waits.

- **Buffet restaurants:** also require reservation in advance. After paying for your meal at the entrance, a Cast Member will accompany you to your table, you hand over the ticket, choose your drink, and from there, you can go to the buffet, serve yourself, and repeat as many times as you want.

- **Quick-service restaurants:** reservations are not accepted at quick-service restaurants. You must order at the counter, your order is prepared on the spot, you pick it up, and then you can sit at any available table. It is the most economical and quick option, especially when using the Mobile Food Order system in the restaurants where it is available.

- **Kiosks, Stands, and Food Trucks:** perfect for a quick break, a snack, or a treat; they are located throughout the park and offer refreshments, ice creams, and some thematic snacks. Prices at these kiosks are more or less standardised, with water and soft drinks costing the same at all of them, €3 and €4 respectively, and snacks and ice creams ranging between €5 and €10.

Additionally, as mentioned in the "Characters" section, two of the restaurants (Plaza Gardens buffet and Auberge de Cendrillon table-service restaurant) offer character dining experiences; and in other restaurants, such as Chez Rémy or Captain Jack's, the atmosphere and décor are an experience in themselves.

For buffet restaurants, table-service restaurants, and character dining experiences, it is necessary to make a reservation (either by phone, through the App, or on the website bookrestaurants.disneylandparis.com/en-gb), even if they are located in your own hotel.

Table reservation becomes available the moment you receive confirmation of your ticket + accommodation reservation for Disney hotel guests (although some may be available a little later). To access them through the App, link your Disney hotel reservation code to your account. If you are staying elsewhere, table booking will open between two and three months before your visit.

If you are interested in a specific restaurant, it is advisable to book a table as soon as you purchase your tickets to the park, knowing that you can always cancel or modify the reservation at any time, free of charge.

If you cannot get a reservation at your preferred restaurant, do not give up and keep an eye on the App, as there are many last-minute modifications and cancellations.

Another option is to book for the approximate number of people in your party, and once at the restaurant, if you need any changes, kindly ask to have your table extended.

This also applies if you have any special requests, such as a table near the windows at Walt's, an American Restaurant, or by the lagoon at the Pirate restaurant. You can even inquire at your hotel reception, where the team will be happy to assist you in getting reservations.

All restaurants offer dishes and menus for children aged 3 to 11, which are increasingly incorporating healthier options. The latter are marked as "Disney Check" children's menus and include less saturated fats and sugars, and at least two portions of fruit and vegetables.

Furthermore, although appetisers and salads are not "magical", many portions are very generous: such as adult-sized pizzas, the Sheriff's Barbecue at Cowboy Cookout Barbecue, or the Fish and Chips at Toad Hall. Considering your family's appetite, if you do not have a Meal Plan, you may be interested in ordering dishes to share.

Lastly, do not hesitate to ask any questions to enhance your experience, inquire about dish ingredients, get the Cast Member's personal recommendation, etc.

Restaurants in Disneyland Park

Main Street, U.S.A.

Table service restaurants and buffets

Walt's, an American Restaurant: this restaurant is dedicated to Walt Disney and his family, and decorated like their family home, with old photos, Victorian furniture, and all kinds of nods to the Disney family and the various corners of the parks.

Reservation is required; if possible, request a table by the window for a better view of Main Street, and, if you time it right, you will see the parades go by.

The food is possibly the best in the park, featuring French and American specialties; if you ask your waiter, they will tell you about the inspiration behind the dishes, especially Walt's favourites. The price corresponds to the quality, with a menu for adults starting from €55, and for children from €30.

Plaza Gardens Buffet: buffet restaurant with open kitchen, in a Victorian style, where you can have encounters with various Disney characters. The food is international and varied, with many options for children, Mickey desserts, and vegan alternatives.

Prices include, in addition to the buffet, visits from various Disney characters during breakfasts and dinners:

- The price of the character breakfast buffet is €42/adult and €36/child.

- For lunch, the buffet costs €45/adult and €25/child, and does not include character visits.

- At dinner time, buffet prices increase to €80/adult and €40/child.

The characters present at breakfasts and dinners are usually four, typically the classic Disney characters like Minnie or Donald; Winnie the Pooh's friends, especially Tigger or Piglet; and some others like Geppetto, Jiminy Cricket, or characters from Peter Pan. In most cases, Mickey Mouse himself joins for dinner. Characters will all visit each table, allow hugs from the children, and take photos with you, although the restaurant is huge and time with each character is limited.

Reservation by phone or app is essential at all times, even if the restaurant voucher is included in your Meal Plan. If you cannot get a reservation at first, but absolutely want to visit, do insist, as there are many last-minute changes and cancellations.

If you are staying at a Disney hotel, in addition to accessing reservations much earlier, you can book the first breakfast slot at 8:15 a.m. Pass through the park access control in a special line, located in the center, about 15-20 minutes before your reservation; and you will be the first visitors to enter Disneyland Paris, even before Extra Magic Time, to enjoy the magic from the very beginning and take spectacular photos in front of Sleeping Beauty Castle completely empty.

The second breakfast slot, at 9:45 a.m., also has its advantages: for Disney hotel guests, as they can make the most of Extra Magic Time, ride some of the available attractions with shorter queues, and enjoy a full breakfast afterwards when other visitors arrive.

Regarding dinner, check the character schedule when booking, as many do not stay until closing, and if you dine very late, you will miss them.

Additionally, during Extra Magic Time, there are not many breakfast options inside the park (except for Cookie Kitchen on Main Street, where you can have coffee or a pastry), so this is a good option if you want to enjoy a full breakfast at that time.

Quick-service restaurants and cafes

Market House Deli: in a corner of Main Street, you will find this American-style takeaway café, with sandwiches, croque-monsieurs, salads, pastries, and cookies, many of them featuring Mickey. With prices ranging from €4 to €9, we recommend them for a satisfying snack or a quick bite while waiting for shows.

Casey's Corner: an American-style café, inspired by the world of baseball, and one of the first Disney shorts ("Casey and the Bat"). Specialising in hot dogs priced around €11, soft drinks, and ice creams, it has a pleasant outdoor terrace to enjoy the good weather.

Cable Car Bake Shop: one of the most beautiful and delightful cafés, where you can have breakfast or a snack with a pastry (approx. €4) and a hot drink. Perfect for rainy days, as it is very cosy, and it connects in the back with the covered passage of Discovery Arcade.

Victoria's Home-Style Restaurant: inspired by a romantic café from the 1980s, it is a nice place for a snack, with sweets like the famous Mickey waffle with Nutella or caramel (€9), accompanied by Viennese hot chocolate or coffee (€4.50). It's a bit hard to find, near Plaza Gardens, just at the end of the street, to the right.

The Gibson Girl Ice Cream Parlour: a "romantic-vintage" style ice cream parlour, offering refreshments, ice creams, Mickey and Minnie sweets, etc.

The Ice Cream Company: a charming ice cream stand, hidden in a side street of Main Street, offering fantasy ice creams and milkshakes (€6), although it is currently closed for renovations.

Cookie Kitchen: a cookie and donut shop-café, perfect for a sweet snack with a hot drink.

Boardwalk Candy Palace: although we also review this small confectionery in our shopping and stores section, if you're craving something sweet and quick, head to their fudge stand, it's addictive!

Fantasyland

Table Service Restaurants

Auberge de Cendrillon: In the heart of Fantasyland, this table-service restaurant offers meals and dinners with Disney princesses. As mentioned in the character section, guests are welcomed by Cinderella and Aurora, along with two mice and two other princesses.

The lunch or dinner menu costs €95 (adults) and €50 (children over 3 years old), including drinks. In both cases, you will be served an appetiser, and you will choose a starter, a main course, and a dessert from the menu (Cinderella's white chocolate slipper is a must). There is also a small selection of wines if you want to accompany your dinner.

The prices at this table-service restaurant are high, but if your little ones are big fans of princesses and meeting them is a "must", this option will save you from the endless queue at the Princess Pavilion. The food is more elaborate than in other restaurants in the park, the decoration is well-kept, and the service is generally attentive, treating your children as if they were royalty.

It is essential to make a reservation, as this is one of the most sought-after restaurants in the park. If you are interested, book as soon as the tables become available (from 6 months before for Disney hotel guests) and keep an eye out for cancellations.

Depending on the season, Auberge de Cendrillon is also available for breakfast, which price ranges between €39 (children over 3 years old) and €59 (adults), on two slots: 8.15 a.m. and 9:45 a.m. As in the case of Plaza Gardens restaurant, the first breakfast sitting allows access to the park even before Extra Magic Time.

Quick Service Restaurants

Pizzeria Bella Notte: A quick-service restaurant with the atmosphere of the Italian trattoria from Lady and the Tramp, perfect for "puppies". Here you will find pasta, lasagne, and pizzas (including Mickey-shaped ones) in menus that range around €17 for adults and €9 for children. In April, a small expansion was inaugurated, themed after the movie "Luca", bringing a piece of Portorosso to this corner of Fantasyland.

Due to its location, it is one of the busiest in the park, and you cannot reserve a table in advance or while ordering; you must find a table after paying for your meal.

Au Chalet de la Marionette: A quick-service restaurant inspired by the adventures of Pinocchio and Geppetto. Like the story itself, it connects the worlds of fairy tales (Fantasyland) and adventures (Adventureland) and has access from both lands, so it's a good idea to stop here for lunch and then cross over to explore the next territory.

The decoration and food inspiration are German, with chicken, currywurst or bratwurst sausages, pretzels, etc. Menus with drinks included range between €16 and €18 for adults and €9 for children.

Toad Hall: This restaurant is one of the least known, perhaps due to its remote location (it's in the "English" part of Fantasyland, between Peter Pan and Meet Mickey), or because it's inspired by another great unknown to the public, the whimsical "The Adventures of Ichabod and Mr. Toad", based on the novel "The Wind in the Willows".

It is the cheapest in the park: Fish and Chips for €12, and for children, €8, with the decoration of a "classic English pub". A good option during peak times and for a budget-friendly meal. Don't miss the restaurant's motto, which prohibits consuming frog legs, the armour in toad format, or the portraits of the conceited Mr. Toad, turned into Van Gogh and the Mona Lisa.

Snacks and Refreshments

March Hare Refreshments: A kiosk for ice creams, soft drinks, and hot beverages, located next to Alice's large teapot (with a surprise inside). There isn't much variety in flavours... all ice creams (€7) are vanilla! but they are undoubtedly the prettiest in the park, decorated with small details from Alice in Wonderland.

The Enchanted Tree: Between Sir Mickey's shop and the teacup attraction, this stall offers refreshments and ice creams, and sometimes sweets for the current celebration. It used to offer "poisoned caramel apples", very fittingly placed next to the apple tree, of course.

The Old Mill: In the old mill, you'll find this stall where you can enjoy a snack or a light meal. Like a good Dutch mill, it usually has Dutch meatballs "Bitterballen", soft drinks, and some Mickey sweets or mini-crepes. You can also find the beautiful Cinderella popcorn chest (€26) and other Disney souvenirs.

Adventureland

Buffet and Table Service Restaurants

Captain Jack's - Pirates Restaurant: This table-service restaurant is one of the most popular, as it is located next to the Pirates of the Caribbean attraction and integrates with it. From the attraction, you can see some of the tables, and from the restaurant, you can dine with a view of the Pirate Lagoon. Set in a buccaneer tavern, its Caribbean-inspired food is very different from the rest of the park (ceviches, fish, curries, soups, and meats...). Your children will love the atmosphere, but the truth is that the food may not be the easiest for them.

The decoration is meticulously crafted, with "wanted" posters of pirates from the saga, characterful waiters, and, occasionally, the visit of Jack Sparrow. The prices of the dishes range from €17 to €38, the adult menu (without drinks) costs €45, and the children's menu, €25.

Agrabah Café: Located in the "Oriental Bazaar" of Adventureland, this buffet is very different from other Disney restaurants. The decoration is spectacular, inspired by "One Thousand and One Nights". The food is full of Moroccan and Middle Eastern flavours, with couscous, salads, spiced chicken, kebabs, and Arabic sweets. The price with drinks included is €40 for adults and €22 for children; payment is made just before entering the restaurant, and reservations are necessary. Due to the type of food, it attracts more adults than children, making it a quiet corner.

Quick Service Restaurants

Hakuna Matata: Inspired by "The Lion King" movie, it is one of the most popular restaurants due to its affordable prices, variety of dishes, and occasional live music. Here you will find fast food with African influences, such as kebabs or spiced chicken, accompanied by rice, salad... The decoration is African-style, with dim lighting, but the tables near the windows and the Timon terrace are pleasant. Adult menus with drinks cost from €16 to €18, and children's menus, €9, and you can reserve the meal through "Mobile Phone Order".

Colonel Hathi's Pizza Outpost: It is a quick-service restaurant, colonial-style, surrounded by vegetation, where you will find pasta and pizzas. The decoration is very well crafted, as it used to be a table-service restaurant. It's inspired by explorers like Indiana Jones, Cousteau, or Livingstone. The price of the menu with drinks is €16, and €9 for the children's menu, where they can choose between Mickey-shaped pasta or pizza... naturally, the "Boss" usually wins the choice! Very pleasant (although crowded) on summer nights, due to the jungle that surrounds its terraces. Look for the two toucans on the central tree!

Snacks and Refreshments

Café de la Brousse (Bush Café): Located between the Agrabah area and the lake surrounding the Robinson's cabin, this small café is not usually very crowded. It offers a few options (chicken bites for €8, or "chocolate claws" for €4.30), suitable for a snack while exploring the jungle; and in summer, some ice creams or slushies.

Cool Post: In this stand on the Silk Road, decorated like an international beverage distribution service, there is a hidden effect that you can show the children. If you open the red soda can, it's full of "ice", and it sounds like you're filling a soda. It offers ice creams, soft drinks, and Mickey waffles.

Frontierland

Table Service Restaurants

Lucky Nugget Saloon: According to legend, the name of this saloon, located in the heart of Frontierland, is due to the "lucky gold nugget" that "Diamond Lil" found during the Gold Rush, allowing her to found this establishment, halfway between a saloon and a cabaret theatre. In this table-service restaurant with menus at €25 for adults and €15 for children, the specialty is burgers and ribs with French fries. Occasionally, they organise shows with characters like Minnie and Goofy or the cowboys from Toy Story. Live music is also present.

Reservations are not accepted at The Lucky Nugget; instead, you queue before entering (it's best to avoid peak hours), and you place your order before having a table. Ask to be seated facing the stage if there's a show, so you don't miss it.

Silver Spur Steakhouse: In this table-service restaurant, set in a Western gentlemen's club, steak is the star, prepared in their open kitchen, as well as some Toy Story-themed desserts. Prices start from €35 for the adult menu, and €25 for the children's menu. Reservations through the App or website are essential.

Quick Service Restaurants

Cowboy Cookout Barbecue: A quick-service restaurant inspired by the American West, offering burgers, chicken, ribs, etc. The menus are quite plentiful and cost between €16 and €18, including drinks, and €9 for children's menus. A unique feature is that all chairs are different, as it was customary in the West for everyone to bring their own chair to town meetings. Occasionally, country music bands play live inside. If the weather is bad, it's a good place to go outside of peak meal times, to enjoy a hot snack by the central fireplace.

Casa de Coco - Family Restaurant (formerly "Fuente Del Oro Restaurant"): This recently renovated quick-service restaurant offers different burritos (€12) and other snack options, as well as churros with Nutella and soft drinks.

Snacks and Refreshments

Overland Trail Cafe: Right in front of Casa de Coco, this new takeaway place gets its inspiration from the Pony Express routes across the Far West. It offers the famous American turkey legs (9 €), alongside sweet treats as churros or popcorn buckets.

Last Chance Cafe: Tex-Mex dishes in this Frontierland restaurant where sheriffs and outlaws "duel" (bullet holes are still visible). The menu offers limited variety, plain nachos (served without sauce), grilled turkey leg and vegan chilli, priced between €6 and €9 drinks excluded. The restaurant's name serves as a clue, just as "last chance".

Discoveryland

Quick Service Restaurants

Café Hyperion: A hamburger restaurant located in a futuristic hangar, presided over by an impressive airship. Menus with drinks cost between €16 and €18 for adults and €9 for children. It is the largest restaurant in the park, with plenty of seating, as it is connected to the Videopolis theatre.

If you are unable to find a table elsewhere, we advise you to approach it and enjoy their short shows while you eat. It has a Mobile Phone Order service, to order your food in advance and save yourself some time. Pay attention, there are also some special features, like a small animatronic bird, or the most futuristic vending machine in the park.

Snacks and Refreshments

Cool Station: Themed sweets (Star Wars or celebration-themed, around €4) and drinks, at this "retro-futuristic" kiosk, illuminated by neon lights and located in front of the Buzz Lightyear attraction.

Walt Disney Studios Restaurants

Table Service and Buffet Restaurants

Bistrot Chez Rémy: A table service restaurant inspired by the famous movie Ratatouille. The decoration is incredible, meticulously recreating Rémy's famous Parisian bistro from the end of the film. From the chairs and tables made of corks and jam jar lids to the lamps (don't miss the bathroom), everything is crafted with imagination and care. Look for Gusteau's famous book and Ego's review in the entrance hall. After the foyer, you'll find yourself "shrunk" to the size of a mouse. Additionally, if children request the chef's signature, Rémy himself will sign their napkin.

You'll need to be vigilant to book through the App; the decor makes it an "attraction" in itself. It's a high-priced restaurant where you can dine à la carte or choose the menu, ranging from €40 to €55 (adults) and €30 (children); the best cuts of meat (at higher prices) are worth it. The service is quite slow, so keep that in mind when planning your schedule.

PYM Kitchen Buffet: A buffet restaurant priced at €45 for adults and €25 for children, drinks included. Located at the beginning of the Avengers Campus and themed after the Antman movie, two huge "grow and shrink" pipes at the entrance give you a hint of what's to come in this lab. The food is either huge or super tiny, served in test tubes and beakers, with a wide variety from rice and burgers to salmon, vegan options, etc. Very fun and very popular, booking is essential!

Quick Service Restaurants:

Stark Factory: A quick-service restaurant inspired by Iron Man's father's facilities. It's self-service; you choose from different counters and pay afterwards. You'll find Italian-style food with pizza by the slice and pasta (approx. €14), as well as some salads and Avengers-themed desserts.

Super Diner: A quick-service diner full of neon lights. It's a bit hidden at the end of the Avengers Campus, but at night, with the illuminated neon lights, it's hard to miss. They offer "shawarmas" (a kind of kebab) for €11, as well as desserts and refreshments. Perfect for a quick bite while watching (if scheduled) the night time Avengers show.

Restaurant en Coulisse: A quick-service restaurant located in Studio 1 (currently under renovation). You'll feel like you're taking a break in a Hollywood studio, surrounded by a thousand sets and neon lights. It's the largest restaurant in the Studios, seating 600 people, with a second floor that opens on busy days—a solution if you don't have a reservation or if the weather makes outdoor dining uncomfortable. The food is American-style, very similar to Café Hyperion, with various burgers and salads. You'll find menus between €16 and €18 for adults and €9 for children.

Food Trucks and Kiosks:

W.E.B. Food Truck: Inspired by Asian cuisine, they offer ramen or noodles bowls (€11), including a vegetarian option, as well as coconut and mango desserts. Located in front of Spiderman W.E.B. Adventures, their snacks are perfect for a quick and inexpensive meal while watching Spiderman perform acrobatics on the rooftop of his attraction.

Laugh'N'Go!: This food truck, which you'll find on the way to the Cars Road Trip attraction, offers some snack options, such as cupcakes or a Lightning McQueen sandwich, with Cars and Pixar decorations and prices between €5 and €8.

FAN-tastic Food Truck: At this spot in the Avengers Campus, you'll find simple hot dogs (including a vegan option) for around €11, as well as snacks, ice creams, or soft drinks.

Ice Cream Creations: The specialty of this "ice cream truck" is the themed "Magnums" decorated with toppings from Toy Story, Cars, or Frozen (€6).

Speciality Ice Cream: In this corner of the Hollywood Boulevard at the Production Courtyard, you can also find fun themed Magnums.

Hep Cat Corner: In Studio 1, this small café offers breakfasts and snacks, including some "themed" sweets like Mickey ice creams or Guardians of the Galaxy cookies (€4).

Toon Studio Catering Co: In the Toon Studio area, you'll find this stand with crepes, Mickey's donuts, and Frozen ice creams (€4).

Finally, in the Ratatouille square, especially between July and September, there is a little market, the **"Rendez-Vous Gourmand",** with several stands where you can find products from different regions of France and the rest of Europe, from Bordeaux to Greece or Switzerland, including a vegan stand. Raclette is a good option to consider.

Disney Village Restaurants

Table service restaurants and buffets.

Annette's Diner: An American restaurant with a 1950s style, where the stars are hamburgers, hot dogs, and milkshakes. It's a table service restaurant where you can eat à la carte (burgers are around €22, with the new Indian Flavours Burger with tandoori spices at €23) or choose from the menu (€25 to €40 for adults, and €16 for children).

In addition to lunches and dinners, they serve hearty American-style breakfasts from 9:30 am to 11:30 am, with pancakes, eggs, sausages... (priced at €15, for both adults and children). Also, during Halloween and Christmas, they have special decorations and menus. This restaurant doesn't accept reservations, so it's best to come outside of peak meal times to avoid queues. It's located in the central square of Disney Village, next to the station and the park entrance, making it a convenient and quick option.

The Steakhouse: A table-service restaurant inspired by 1950s Chicago, offering various grilled meat cuts, salads, etc. Like in all table-service restaurants, you can order à la carte (perhaps the highest-priced menu in the Village, but also of the best quality) or choose from the menu, with prices starting from €35 for adults and €25 for children.

La Grange at Billy Bob's Country Western Saloon: On the second floor of the Billy Bob's Saloon Bar is this Tex Mex buffet. It offers dinner services with a selection of meats, salads, side dishes, and a great variety of themed desserts, priced at €40 for adults and €22 for children up to 11 years old (children under 3 do not pay admission). From the gallery upstairs, guests can watch performances in the bar on the lower floor. Reservations are necessary and can be made at the reception, through the App, or on the Disneyland Paris website.

Rosalie: The former Café Mickey in Disney Village has recently been converted into this modern and bright brasserie, offering French-inspired cuisine from morning to night, including typical fish dishes, seafood, and *escargots* (snails). Guests can order à la carte or opt for a set menu (from €25 at noon). You can also start the day with an "express" or "gourmand" breakfast (€8.59 - €12) or order something to take away.

Quick service restaurants

Billy Bob's Country Western Saloon: An American-style bar, with a slightly more adult feel, where you can enjoy soft drinks and some snack options (chicken wings, ribs, desserts...) à la carte or as a set menu (€15). On Fridays and Saturdays, and until 2 am, there are live performances or music.

Earl of Sandwich: A quick-service restaurant that is very easy to find, as it is located right next to the hot air balloon, on the edge of the lake. It specialises in large sandwiches and wraps (€9), much better than those in the park, and is a good option for something casual on the way to the hotel or before heading back to the airport. It opens at 8 am and closes at 11 pm. Breakfasts are also served, slightly cheaper than in the park, and perfect to take away before entering. The service is very fast, but if you're in a hurry or ordering after the fireworks (when it usually fills up), you can use the "Click and Collect" service on their website, make your order and pick it up to go.

https://commandes.earlofsandwich.fr/home/places

Starbucks: Although this chain may not be tailored for children, it's very likely that adults will need a good coffee to face the day. During peak seasons, this establishment gets crowded and the queue can make you lose valuable minutes, so if you're staying at the Cheyenne or Santa Fe hotel, it's much better to go there than to the Village.

Five Guys: In this famous American chain, the specialty is made to order burgers (from €10, and children's meals, €7) with ingredients of your choice from their wide range of options. They also offer hot dogs, sandwiches, French fries, and milkshakes, for the complete American experience.

New York Style Sandwiches: A quick-service restaurant with American-style menus priced between €10 and €15 for adults, and €9 for children. The selection is very basic, only recommended for a quick snack or if you're craving a Mickey ice cream or dessert available on the menu.

Rainforest Cafe: A quick-service international style restaurant, set in the jungle, with interactive games, animatronics, and a decoration full of animals and vegetation. It will appeal to little explorers, and parents will appreciate their slightly more elaborate food than in the park, ranging from salads (€20) to pasta (€25) or meat dishes (€30).

McDonald's: Classic burgers and salads accompanied by fries and your favourite drink. In addition, for something quick or a budget breakfast, they have a McDonald's Pick-up point.

Vapiano: A chain of Mediterranean-Italian restaurants, with a modern and bright style, focusing on fresh pasta, pizza made to order, and open kitchen. The quality-price ratio is better compared to other pasta and pizza options in the park, and the salads can be very appealing after several days of fast food. However, the wait can be endless (especially in the case of pasta made to order by the "Vapianisti"). If you're in a hurry, order a pizza or lasagne (they provide a device to notify you once it's ready). You can check the menu and prices on the chain's website (www.vapiano.fr), and even, in the "A emporter" section, place your order via mobile.

The Royal Pub (formerly King Ludwig's Castle): Recreates the quintessential English pub, serving British-inspired food, as well as burgers (approx. €23), sandwiches, and snacks, that you can pair with a wide selection of beers (with Happy Hour from 5:30 to 7 pm). You can also have a hearty English breakfast (€24), which includes sausages, bacon, etc., available all day.

Sports Bar: An American-style pub, with screens airing sports events, where you can enjoy drinks or beers (approx. €7), but also some snacks, sandwiches, or even Mickey beignets and pizzas (€12). It's not the most child-friendly atmosphere unless it coincides with an "epic" game of their favourite team, etc.

At the Marne - la Vallée - Chessy train station, next to the RER accesses, you'll also find some points like **Relay, Petit Monoprix**, and **Pret a Manger**, where you can stock up on drinks and snacks to take to the park, as well as sandwiches and salads, for approximately €6.

Water, Refill Service, and Alcoholic Beverages

Tap water, as mentioned in the "Luggage" section, is free. There are drinking water fountains throughout the park where you can refill your bottles, and restaurants are required to serve it upon customer request.

No bar or restaurant in the park allows "refills", refilling your drink. It's not because they're more stingy than Americans, where it's very common, but because French legislation on sugar consumption control prohibits it, even more so in a park especially for children.

However, Disneyland Paris is one of the few Disney parks that serves alcoholic beverages, and you'll find beer and a small selection of wines in many of its restaurants, as well as some cocktails or the Casa de Coco Margarita slushie.

Mobile Food Order

At quick-service restaurants, advance booking isn't an option, but at several of them, you can pre-order your food and drinks. This can be done through the "Mobile Food Order" system, allowing you to pick up your order without waiting. However, please note that this service is not yet available for Meal Plans. To order via Mobile Food Order, go to the Disneyland Paris app and select the restaurant in the Food > Order food and drink section. Choose your meal and a time to pick it up.

If you bought the annual pass, you can use the discount at this point and then proceed to check out. Go to the restaurant at the selected time and click on the confirmation email, "I'm here!". You'll only need to pick up your order at the "Mobile Food Order" counter without waiting, either to take away or to consume in the restaurant. This service is available at the following quick-service restaurants:

- In Disneyland Park: Casa de Coco, Casey's Corner, Café Hyperion, Last Chance Café, and Hakuna Matata Restaurant.

- In Walt Disney Studios: Restaurant En Coulisse

Allergies and Celiac Disease

Food allergies and intolerances are becoming more prevalent and concerning, a matter that Disneyland Paris takes very seriously. All restaurants provide menus listing the main allergens present in all dishes they serve. The policy in this regard has recently changed, and they no longer offer Natama allergen-free menus that were available until now, although they are working on new menus. Additionally, changes to dishes cannot be made, nor can it be ensured that there is no cross-contamination between the different ingredients in the restaurants.

In all hotels and most restaurants in the parks that serve breakfast, special products for visitors with food allergies can be found (following the same policy, the absence of traces is not guaranteed). They are not available in the buffet; you will have to ask a staff member to provide them to you.

Therefore, if your allergy is mild and you tolerate traces, you can consult the allergen menu and choose from it. Upon arriving at the restaurant, approach staff and inform them of your type of intolerance or allergy. If you make a reservation, indicate the type of allergy beforehand, to ensure a smoother and more accommodating service.

However, if your allergy is severe and you cannot tolerate traces, it is advisable to bring food from home (always in plastic containers and avoiding sharp utensils). For this, the easiest thing is to book an Airbnb with a kitchen where you can prepare meals (or a cabin at Davy Crockett Ranch if you prefer to stay at a Disney hotel and take advantage of the EMT). Keep in mind that most Disney hotels do not provide a fridge in the rooms.

Don't forget to bring a medical certificate certifying the allergy, to avoid inconveniences when accessing the park with your meal. Additionally, review all your doctor's prescriptions, such as antihistamines, epi-pens, allergy identification, etc., as well as medical justifications to pass through the luggage control at the airport.

Other Dietary Needs

Vegan Food

All Disney restaurants offer vegan options, although there is limited variety in quick-service and table-service restaurants, only one or two options in each. Buffets, especially at breakfast, have many vegan alternatives, and of course, many fruit options.

In Disneyland Park, the best option is buffet restaurants, especially Agrabah Café, with its salads and couscous, and Plaza Gardens Restaurant, where Disney character encounters are scheduled during breakfast and dinner.

In Walt Disney Studios Park, there are other options, such as the buffet restaurant, PYM Kitchen, or vegan alternatives from the Food Trucks, from ramen to hot dogs. In the "Rendez-Vous Gourmand" area, there is a vegan stand, "The Vegan Gourmet Food Stand", which offers a delicious vegan chocolate cake and a vegan Yule log cake.

Halal and Kosher Food

All table-service and buffet restaurants in the parks, Disney accommodations, and Disney Village offer certified halal and kosher food options, upon request. To order them, simply call 01 60 30 40 50 (French number, with local call rate) at least 48 hours in advance.

Note that orders placed between Friday at 2:00 p.m. and Monday at 9:00 a.m. cannot be guaranteed after 48 hours, so you will need to call at least Friday morning to ensure it is not too late

Shopping at Disneyland Paris

Shopping and Family Budget

Disneyland is a shopping paradise for Disney fans, filled with stores offering thousands of details and memories at various price ranges. Want some Minnie ears with glitter, a unicorn horn, and a bridal veil? It's a real request... and voilà! Your wish is granted! Disneyland also features thousands of items from Marvel, Star Wars, and Pixar, catering to both children and adults.

Moreover, many of the stores are "attractions in themselves", corners of the park with spectacular decorations or magical effects that you won't want to miss.

It's important to manage these temptations wisely and establish a "limit" on purchases for the whole family in advance. To set it, you'll need to consider not only your budget but also the age of the children, with a limit that they understand and accept beforehand—this will save you many tantrums! There are many options; it could be a single gift at the end of the trip (so they can choose what they liked most within your budget) or a small one each day if you're not visiting the parks again.

For older children, it's a good opportunity to explain the value of money by setting a monetary limit. If the trip is planned in advance and they expect it, they can "earn" their budget through small extra tasks at home (outside their routine, understanding that not all responsibilities come with a reward).

As mentioned in the "Luggage" section, all shops and restaurants accept Visa, MasterCard, and American Express (confirm with your bank beforehand that international charges aren't blocked). It's also advisable to carry cash for any incidents.

Always check the back of receipts from the park and Disney Village as they sometimes contain gift vouchers or discounts for subsequent purchases.

A little-known detail is that returns are accepted (you'll need to present the purchase receipt, and the item must be in the same condition, packaging, tags, etc.). If your little one changes their mind, or if you try it at the hotel and it doesn't convince you, no problem—they'll refund the money in the same payment method you used. Likewise, if you encounter any problems with an item, you can contact the store's after-sales service via email at dlp.guest.communication@disneylandparis.com.

If your children, like ours, aren't big fans of browsing stores (unless they can leave with their hands full), they'll still enjoy the most special ones. Those that are "attractions in themselves" that are worth seeing; you'll find them marked with a ★.

If you don't want to carry shopping bags around all day, you can ask to have them sent from the store to the reception of your Disney hotel or to Disney Village. This service is free (although some shops are starting to ask for a minimum of €50 in purchases to use it) and is available only before 3 p.m. You can also, within or outside that schedule, ask them to hold the bags in the store for later pick-up.

Moreover, children can donate their old toys at store checkout counters and give them a second life through the park's solidarity campaigns, although it's difficult to take them there for practical reasons.

When is the best time to visit the stores? There are many recommended times to do your shopping route: first thing in the morning when they're less crowded; before lunch (when attraction queues are at their peak), or late in the day when you can't ride attractions anymore. The stores on Main Street close nearly an hour after the park's official closing time, but keep in mind that after the fireworks, all visitors pass through Main Street towards the exit.

Finally, don't forget to consider the restrictions on liquids and merchandise for the plane; you wouldn't want to have to leave your treasures at the baggage checkpoint!

Disneyland Park Stores

Main Street, U.S.A.:

On the left sidewalk, between the main street and Liberty Arcade, we find:

The Storybook Store: in a corner of Main Street, we find this beautiful spot. At the entrance, Tigger welcomes you from a glass counter, surrounded by books, comics, stationery items, and framed prints. The store is lovely and decorated with Disney characters "studying", some of them a bit hidden, like Cinderella's mouse Jack-Jack.

Emporium: this store brings together a large collection of Disney merchandise under a glass dome dedicated to great inventors. If you look closely, there's a system of rails and little carts on the ceiling, which was used to move cash from one side of the store to the other. If you only have one day and no time for shopping but want to take home a souvenir, this is the best option, as it boasts a wide assortment and is the last to close.

Disney&Co ★: a beautiful "old-fashioned" toy store, full of dolls and plush toys, where Mickey and Donald welcome you from a hot air balloon. Each section is inspired by a corner of the circus, including funhouse mirrors to look at yourself!

Dapper Dan's Hair Cut: it's an authentic barbershop, inspired by Walt Disney's father, a barber by profession, where, by appointment, you can experience something different and leave with a haircut. Prices start from €26, a little less for shaves. The salon chairs are original from the time, as is the collection of cups we can find on the shelves. In fact, the manufacturing date is displayed on several of the items, dating back to the early 19th century. On the storefront, there are two signs, for adults and children, where you can see your reflection against the glass, complete with a comical moustache. It's worth at least a peek inside to see the decoration. They are open for limited hours, but if it's closed, you can still catch a glimpse from inside the Emporium store, where you can also schedule an appointment.

Lily's Boutique: this store brings together a selection of home items (such as dishes, cushions, cutlery...), as well as jams and teas inspired by the famous Wonderland tea party. The name of the boutique is a tribute to Walt Disney's wife: Lillian, known as "Lily". Like Walt's restaurant, the interior recalls the Disney family home, carefully decorated and full of memories of their life together and their travels through Europe.

On the other hand, on the right sidewalk, between Main Street and Discovery Arcade, you will find:

Ribbons and Bows Hat Shop: initially, this was a charming hat and headwear shop, which has now made way for a great selection of Loungefly backpacks (around €70), with incredible designs for both children and adults. You can also get lost among thousands of accessories, like Pandora jewellery charms, Minnie ears, cosmetics, and a small Christmas corner.

New Century Notions Flora's Unique Boutique: this store represents old warehouses, with a range of clothing, accessories, ears, etc.

It features a special detail; if you pick up the old phone on the wall (just to the left of the cash register), you can hear the conversations of the locals, which intertwine with those from Dapper Dan's Haircut phone and Market House Deli.

Boardwalk Candy Palace: in this store, decorated in the style of an old-fashioned confectionery, you'll find the park's most classic sweets and candies: lollipops, cotton candy, popcorn, macarons, and a small stand of cookies and American fudge (an addictive toffee-like sweet, irresistible!); as well as Rémy and Gusteau's recipe books.

Disney Clothiers: the largest selection of clothing for children and babies, with practically every possible Disney character.

Main Street Motors: if Disney Clothiers is focused on children, Main Street Motors does the same with adults, with a wide selection of clothing, Loungefly accessories, etc. At least peek into the storefront to see Cruella de Vil riding her convertible.

Disneyana: Speaking of prints, you can find plenty in this gallery, and even a booth where artists go to work on their art... If you miss one of these stores and fancy a print for your home, you can find many at The Disney Gallery, in Disney Village, at the park exit.

Harrington's Fine China & Porcelains: this store, specialising in glassware, features a spectacular glass dome, which creates a curious acoustic effect: If you stand on the marks at one end, you can perfectly hear the conversation on the other side of the store.

Fantasyland

La Boutique du Château (the Castle store) ★: entering the Castle, on the right, you'll find this little shop, where it's Christmas all year round! Its Christmas ornaments are a lovely detail for any family tree and fill this store with charm with its stained-glass windows and decorated ceilings. Note that "snow globes" are difficult to transport by plane: they can't go in carry-on luggage due to current liquid restrictions, and they can break even in checked baggage.

Merlin l'Enchanteur ★: located opposite the Castle Boutique, Merlin's Wizard store is dedicated to the world of Crystal with thousands of figurines, jewellery, and glassware (and Cinderella's shoe collection, of course). Sometimes there's a glass artisan who, with a blowtorch and goggles, shapes wands and figures, undoubtedly the most surprising thing for your little wizard apprentices.

La Chaumière des Sept Nains ★: crossing the Castle, on the left, you'll find this store set in Snow White's tale, with everything little princesses could wish for: costumes, figurines, and dolls of all kinds. The store is very beautiful and represents everything from the Evil Queen's rooms to the Seven Dwarfs' "beds".

The elements adorning its showcases, like old books or glass, were purchased by Imagineers in antique shops, like many others in the park, understanding that the European visitor was more accustomed to seeing antiques and would want a "real" flavour.

La Confiserie des Trois Fées ★: nothing to do with Flora, Fauna, and Merryweather's disastrous birthday cake; in this store, the three fairy godmothers have performed real magic with their wands to fill their trees and wooden beams with spectacular candies and sweets, and if you approach the fireplace, you'll see them fluttering in it.

Sir Mickey's Boutique ★: inspired by the movies "Mickey and the Beanstalk" and "The Brave Little Tailor", this plush and costume store is surrounded by a little garden, where the beanstalk has grown out of control and crept into the store, while another of the rooms, "La Ménagerie du Royaume", is inspired by a jousting tournament. Don't miss the giant peeking through the store's ceiling! In this store, you can also enjoy Fantasyland's face painting.

La Bottega di Gepetto: as a good toy maker, Geppetto has gathered in his workshop a selection of rag puppets, plush toys, and toys, especially from Pinocchio, Toy Story...

Adventureland

Les Trésors de Scheherazade: Inspired by a bazaar from One Thousand and One Nights, or perhaps Ali Baba's Cave, with its lighting, colours, and swords hanging from the ceiling. An enormous camel presides over the center of the store, filled with costumes, jewellery...

Le Coffre du Capitaine: This is the "treasure cave" if your children are fans of corsairs and buccaneers. Located next to the "Captain Jack's" restaurant, it features many themed items from the attraction; even the weathervane is a pirate! Sometimes characters like Hook, Smee, etc., appear on the balcony of the first floor, and during Halloween, it becomes "especially terrifying" with pumpkins and souvenirs of The Nightmare Before Christmas.

The Curious Giraffe ★: The unique thing about the store is... the Giraffe! The little ones will be amazed by its animated head eating the straw ceiling of this store, specialised in merchandise from The Lion King and Aladdin.

Temple Traders Boutique and Indiana Jones Adventure Outpost: Next to the Indiana Jones attraction, and near the Colonel Hathi restaurant, respectively, these huts offer many souvenirs (T-shirts, plush toys, etc.) from The Lion King, and, of course, items from the famous archaeologist.

Frontierland:

Thunder Mesa Mercantile Building: Inspired by the gold rush warehouses of the Old West, this warehouse gathers the largest collection of housewares (cups, glasses, bowls, etc.), as well as pet items and toys, featuring many Disney characters, but especially those from the "New World", like the cowboys from Toy Story, the heroines from Encanto, or Coco. Fans of Nightmare Before Christmas will find the store full of its products during the Halloween season.

Discoveryland:

Star Traders ★: At the exit of the Star Tours attraction, you can't miss this souvenir shop. Themed around Star Wars, it's the ideal place for little and big "geeks": all kinds of items from the saga, clothing, costumes (the Ewoks ones are great, and the Darth Vader masks that modify the voice), Star Wars face painting, a workshop where you can assemble your own lightsaber and even a station to customise mini-droids. The little padawan enthusiasts will go crazy, just bear in mind that the prices can also be "astronomical" (lightsabers around €40, etc).

Constellations: Next to the Buzz Lightyear Laser Blast attraction, this shop features souvenirs from this Space Ranger and his little green men, along with other "Disney" aliens like Stitch or Wall-E, many Marvel details, and, of course, Mickey, Minnie, etc. It's best to visit at night when the ceiling lighting is much prettier.

Walt Disney Studios Stores

Chez Marianne (Souvenirs de Paris): Located in the Studios, in the Ratatouille area, it's entirely inspired by a Parisian confectionery. It's filled with lollipops and cookies, but visitors will also find kitchen gifts for Mini-Chefs, Paris souvenirs, shoulder plushies of Remy...

Mission Equipment ★: It's the most technological of Disney's stores, dedicated to the world of Spider-Man and "Stark Industries", showcases all kinds of gadgets, clothing, dolls... The most sought-after item for little Spider-Man fans is the Spider-Bot ("Tracey" from the Spidey Super Team), a spider-like robot that kids can control remotely, make it fight against another one, customise it with shells, etc.

Beware, without customization, they already cost around €70 each, and to make them fight, you need two, so it's quite an "investment". They also have "web shooters" that help score more points in the Spider-Man W.E.B. attraction and include different "Marvel" features, like Iron Man's lights. Be cautious with souvenirs from any Marvel or Star Wars store: if you purchase a toy that looks like a real weapon, it won't be permitted in your carry-on luggage. A "lightsaber" is an exception, of course.

Animation Boutique: (currently under renovation) In this store, the protagonists are animation figures, present in thousands of details in Arribas crystal, Christmas decorations, tiaras, and small jewellery, especially from the Studios' protagonists: Frozen characters, Pixar, and of course, Mickey.

Les Légendes d'Hollywood: In this huge store, inspired by a Hollywood set, there's a varied selection of Disney, Pixar, Marvel, and Star Wars merchandise, including customizable lightsabers that we saw at Star Traders.

Toy Story Playland Boutique: this small store in the Toy Story land, located in a toy barrel, is the home for all characters from the famous saga.

Tower Hotel Gifts: In a corner of the Tower of Terror, you'll find this store, specialised in exclusive souvenirs from the Tower experience: T-shirts, door knockers, bellboy hats... as well as Nightmare Before Christmas and other Disney "villains" details. You can also purchase your "On-Ride" photo here (visit our Photopass section to learn more).

Walt Disney Studios Store: (currently closed for renovation) In this huge store on the Studios' Front Lot, you used to find a wide variety of Disney merchandise of all kinds, souvenirs, and trinkets; as well as Photopass+ services.

Hollywood Jewel Box: If you're a Pandora charms collector, don't miss this little corner, which offers all imaginable Disney jewellery, including some limited editions.

Studio Photo: In this space, next to Studio Services, in the Front Lot, you can print photos and purchase Photopass+, and some other photography items, like disposable cameras, camera accessories, or photo frames. They also sell souvenirs, ears, trinkets, autograph books, and some baby items, as it's also close to the Baby Care Centre.

Stores in Disney Village

The shops in Disney Village offer extended opening hours, and close later into the evening. This makes them a convenient option if you prefer to make the most of your time on attractions and shows and then take a stroll through the Village shops after the park has closed.

The Disney Store ★: The decoration of this store is spectacular, with old airplanes and spaceships moving around piloted by classic Disney characters. It brings together a varied selection of merchandise and toys, especially plush toys of all characters, but also customizable lightsabers, a droid assembly station, and other small Star Wars modelling items...

A feature that children will love is the option to create their own Mr. Potato Head in the Toy Story section, even with Disney and Star Wars accessories. As part of the renovation of Disney Village, The Disney Store will close to make way for the new 'Disney Wonders' store. Meanwhile, The Disney Store closes at midnight, so, as we say, you can visit it after the fireworks. Don't miss the decoration of the ceiling; it is worth the visit.

World of Disney ★: A huge hot air balloon piloted by Pluto and Mickey presides over this store with a very wide range of clothing, figurines, ear hats, etc. It boasts one of the longest opening hours in the area (from 9 am to 1 am, although it varies by season) and since it's located outside the park, you can also visit it when the park is closed.

The Disney Gallery: The collector's paradise! All kinds of souvenirs, from pins to figurines and sculptures. Additionally, it offers a large selection of prints and the "Art on Demand" service: a screen where you can choose from a thousand print options, select the format and type of printing, and have it sent to your home by mail within two weeks.

There are prints ranging from about €18 (+ €6 shipping with tracking number) to infinity, as you can even add the frame, which will consequently multiply the cost and shipping.

Disney Fashion: Limited editions of Disney clothing, and even the option to customise garments in its Atelier section. The children's store (Disney Fashion Jr.) is closed for renovations; currently, the entire collection is in Disney Fashion. Additionally, as part of the renovation plans for Disney Village, Disney Fashion and Disney Gallery will merge to become a large fashion retail outlet., and Disney Fashion Jr. will close to become a Disney homeware shop.

The LEGO Store: If your children are fans of the world's most popular construction game, you can't miss this store, decorated with huge LEGO models and mosaics. It boasts a large collection, from the most impressive (and impressively expensive) Star Wars and Harry Potter sets to our favourite part of the game: the possibility of buying various bricks and unleashing your imagination (starting at €10 for the small container).

To practise, there is a large central area for free play in the store, which is usually bustling with children building stuff; and other stands where you can make your own minifigure, or even your own LEGO mosaic portrait (approximately €100).

Free Souvenirs and Outlets

If your budget is tight but you still want a small memento of your visit, here are some ideas for magical freebies to take from the park.

At City Hall and at the hotel receptions, they give out badges and buttons for free (supposedly only to children) commemorating some celebrations, as was the case during the 30th anniversary of Disneyland Paris. Sometimes stickers are also available, which will make your children feel like "VIPs".

If you are celebrating a birthday during your visit, you can request a special birthday badge, both at the hotel reception and at City Hall or Studio Services. Note that this badge has magical powers! With it, Cast Members will congratulate the wearer all day long and may even offer a special treat at restaurants and attractions. If it doesn't coincide with a birthday, they also give them out for anniversaries or even for the first visit to the park.

During the pandemic, this tradition was suspended, and now it depends on the available stock at any given time. Speaking of birthdays, don't forget to visit our "Celebrate a Birthday" section for tips on getting small treats.

If you eat at Toad Hall (the most affordable restaurant in the park), ask the waiters for a new copy of the "Toad Hall Telegraph". At "Animation Academy" in the Studios, as we mentioned in the lands section, you will be taught to draw your own Disney character, which you can take home as a souvenir, as well as the driver's licence for the Autopia by Avis attraction, or, at Together! Pixar show, the screenplay.

Pin trading is an activity carried out by some Cast Members (they wear a Pin Trader badge) in all Disney parks. It consists of exchanging a Disney pin you have with them, being able to choose any from their board or lanyard.

To acquire pins to exchange, we recommend looking for lots on eBay and similar sites (it is essential that these pins are official, bearing the Disney © on the back). There are special places for this exchange, such as Harrington's, or the Pueblo Trading Post in Frontierland (in the Frontierland theatre area), which opens on weekends and during special Pin Trading events among visitors.

If you are looking for something extra, shop at the Disney Village outlet, located next to the LEGO Store, where you will find products from other seasons, discontinued, and discounted, with considerable savings. Speaking of the LEGO store, you can request the free "LEGO Passport" there and get it stamped at the Disneyland Village store.

There are also two shopping centers nearby, whose nearest train station is about 10 minutes away by RER A train from the park.

- The "Val d'Europe" shopping centre offers a variety of shops, including a Primark store full of Disney clothing and accessories, for adults, children, and babies, from T-shirts and sweatshirts to notebooks and ear headbands.

- "La Vallée Village Chic Outlet", boasts many luxury stores at outlet prices.

Visiting in Bad Weather

In Paris, rain is very common in all seasons, and in winter, temperatures can drop below zero, sometimes resulting in snow. The good news is that the park is well prepared for such conditions, and operates "almost" normally on those days. You will find many indoor attractions and adapted versions of shows, and the queues will be minimal; it's a good opportunity to ride your favourite attractions multiple times. Tell the kids that "Elsa" is in charge today and to be prepared in case it snows!

If you are travelling in cold months, take the climate into account when choosing the hotel: look for an option closer to the park to facilitate transfers in cold and rainy weather, and consider those with a heated pool.

Additionally, the New York - The Art of Marvel and Newport hotels have almost all their pathways indoors. The Sequoia does not, but it remains a "Christmas" option due to its spaces and fireplace, while Davy Crockett Ranch and Cheyenne are better options in good weather since almost all their trails are outdoors. The Santa Fe hotel is the most economical option, particularly recommended in autumn and winter, as it lacks air conditioning for the summer months.

Check the weather forecast to adjust your trip. If you are going to be there for several days, plan for the "drier" day fireworks, outdoor parades, and open-air attractions; and for the rainiest ones, indoor attractions, table service restaurants (trying to adapt reservations), or character meals, and visits to the shops.

If you don't have a reservation at any restaurant, a good option is to go to the Hyperion restaurant; it provides plenty of indoor space, and you can entertain the kids with shorts or a show at the Videopolis theatre.

Parades are only cancelled if the rain is quite heavy or there is a storm. However, once they start, they proceed regardless of the weather conditions. Check the App, and you will see if there are cancellations or any changes in them.

The best places to see the afternoon parade indoors are: from the central kiosk of Town Square (except at Christmas, when the Christmas tree blocks the view), from the porch of the Plaza Gardens restaurant, and even through the windows of Walt's restaurant if you dine late and your budget allows it.

Fireworks also take place despite the rain, although perhaps a shorter and "blurrier" version, and they are only cancelled in extreme weather or a strong storm, for the comfort and safety of visitors.

Packing for bad weather

Germans, experts in cold weather have a saying, "there is no bad weather, only the wrong clothing": Bring waterproof shoes and coat, thermal undershirt, hat, a neck warmer, and gloves, a small but sturdy umbrella, and if heavy rains threaten, a poncho that covers both you and your backpack. In the parks, you can also purchase ponchos for about €12, but the quality-price ratio is not the best.

Make sure your backpacks are waterproof to carry documentation, phone, chargers, etc., or at least provide a waterproof inner pocket.

For children, the best option is waterproof pants or a jumpsuit that can be worn over clothing and sturdy shoes. Some wear rain boots since they go from puddle to puddle, but it's not comfortable for walks.

If you're unsure about footwear, at least use a waterproofing spray (available at Decathlon and Amazon) to help protect their sneakers. You can do the same for jackets, stroller covers, backpacks, etc. Again, don't forget to include hats, neck warmers, and gloves for everyone (for adults, it is recommended to choose the kind that allows you to use the touchscreen of your mobile phone).

It doesn't hurt to add a couple of **extra socks** and even a change of clothes and shoes in the backpack if the day is very rainy; there's nothing more uncomfortable than spending the day on wet clothing or having to return to the hotel for a change.

A great ally on cold days is **hand warmer patches** or packets, which will provide you with several hours of warmth instantly. If you're going to carry them on the plane, carefully read the instructions for use, as they should not be classified as dangerous or flammable goods. If packaged as liquids, they must comply with the boarding limitations for liquids. Speaking of liquids, some **water fountains** may be closed to avoid issues with ice, but you'll always find covered ones open, such as the ones at the Arcades. You may also consider switching one of your water bottles to a hot beverage bottle.

All these "just in case" items can take up a lot of space and weight, so if you're not using a stroller, we recommend using the park lockers and leaving the "spares" there; the lockers cost €7 per day, but they will save you a lot of weight during the day.

In the "Travelling with Babies" section, we remind you of necessary accessories for the stroller during bad weather, such as the rain cover or sleeping bag, but even if you're not bringing one, your children will appreciate a fleece blanket, especially during parades or shows.

Covered Passages and Tours

In the park, there are some covered passageways and passages through which you can quickly reach different areas, not only helping you to avoid crowds but also keeping you dry along the way.

Additionally, these galleries have benches and restrooms, where you can take a break, rest, dry off, change your children's clothes, etc. Don't hesitate to use them; your kids will be impressed with your "superhero" knowledge of the park.

From the central plaza of Main Street USA, you can find two passageways parallel to the main street, leading to the Castle Square. Liberty Arcade (to the left of Main Street) and Discovery Arcade (to the right).

- If you choose Liberty Arcade and, at the end of this hallway, turn slightly to the left, you will connect with another covered passageway that also leads to Frontierland.

- At the end of this second passageway, if you turn left again, you will see the Lucky Nugget Saloon. From there, you can shelter under its porches, and then, in those of the Last Chance Café and the Silver Spur, on your way to Phantom Manor, whose queue is covered.

- On the other hand, if you continue straight after the second passageway, you will pass under the wooden fort of Frontierland, connecting with the next little-known covered hallway, which will take you to the Agrabah Marketplace in Adventureland.

  The marketplace is outdoors, but if you walk along its left side, a few metres away, you will find the last passageway, which will take you under arcades to Pirates of the Caribbean and Peter Pan.

These galleries or corridors are not only ideal for sheltering from heavy rain but also very useful on days of high attendance, since some are unknown by the general public and will easily take you from one point to another in the park. A great trick to repeat your favourite attractions on the last day!

Covered Attractions and Shows

Regarding indoor attractions or those with queues under a roof, we've previously mentioned Phantom Manor, but being Paris' climate so unstable, with over 100 rainy days a year, there are many other options where the waiting line and the ride are sheltered. As the crowds decrease, you might even be able to ride some of them over and over again!

Covered Attractions	
Disneyland Park - Fantasyland	**Disneyland Park - Discoveryland**
Peter Pan's Flight	Hyperspace Mountain
Snow White and the Seven Dwarfs	Star Tours
Les Voyages de Pinocchio	Buzz Lightyear's Laser Blast
Mad Hatter's Tea Cups	Star Port
Le Carousel de Lancelot (Partly)	Mickey's Philharmagic
Princess Pavilion	Les Mystères du Nautilus
Meet Mickey	**Walt Disney Studios**
Disneyland Park - Adventureland	Crush's Coaster
Pirates of the Caribbean	Spider-Man W.E.B Adventure
Indiana Jones and the Temple of Peril	Ratatouille
Aladdin's Enchanted Passage	Avenger's Assemble: Flight Force
Disneyland Park - Frontierland	Frozen: A Musical Invitation
Phantom Manor	Mickey and the Magician
Rustler's Shooting Gallery (additional fee)	Stitch Live!
Frontierland Theatre: The Lion King	Together! A Pixar Musical Adventure

Travelling in Hot Weather

Although it's not typical in Paris, the months of **July and August** can be hot, with occasional heatwaves. If that's the case, don't forget to hydrate frequently, paying special attention to children. Also, make use of a hat or cap, sunglasses, sunscreen with SPF 50, and refreshing wipes, as well as American visitors from Florida, true specialists in travelling in hot weather, even bring towels called Frogg Toggs / Chilly Pad, which instantly cool you down. If you're travelling with very young children or babies, it's a good idea to bring a handheld or stroller fan and a parasol for waiting in lines or under the sun.

It's the perfect time to see **indoor shows**, where you'll be cool thanks to the air conditioning, such as Mickey and the Magician, The Lion King musical, Frozen: A Musical Invitation, or Pixar Together. The indoor attractions with **sheltered queues** recommended in the previous section will be your best allies, not forgetting others where you might get a little wet, like Pirates of the Caribbean, Cars Road Trip, or Big Thunder Mountain.

Travelling with Babies

As we mentioned at the beginning of the guide, although it's most advisable to travel with children aged 5 or older, there's no problem if you decide to travel with younger children, due to personal preference, budget constraints, or if your little one is the youngest of several siblings; Disneyland Paris is a park for children, and although there will be attractions they can't ride, there are many other options to enjoy with them.

Additionally, it's worth noting that children up to three years old don't pay the entrance fee at the park, nor for accommodation or meals. This is as long as they share their parents' plate in table-service or quick-service restaurants, while in a buffet, they can have their own plate without any problem. So, here's a point in favour of bringing your child under 3 to Disney, or even celebrating their third birthday there, as long as the first day of the reservation is before their birthday.

You can even order a personalised cake (which costs €35 in many restaurants) or a surprise gift in the room. Don't miss our "Celebrating a Birthday" section with all the available possibilities.

Disneyland Paris is a park designed for families, where thrilling rides are not the main focus. There's always a gentle alternative to enjoy with a baby while the rest of the family rides roller coasters (check it out at our "Divide and Conquer" chapter).

Additionally, as we saw in the "Quick Access to Attractions" section, don't forget to use "Rider Switch" (or "Baby Switch"), as well as the Single Rider line, so you don't miss out on all the attractions. For babies, encounters with characters, parades, and shows are perfect, full of music, colour, and movement.

Throughout this chapter, we'll give you tips and tricks to make the trip more comfortable and peaceful for both babies and adults.

Strollers and Baby Carriers

A **stroller** is essential when travelling with babies and can be very useful even if your children no longer use it regularly: in Disneyland, you walk many kilometres a day, and the little ones will appreciate a break from walking or a place to sit in parades, character lines…. It will also provide extra storage space to carry their things without carrying them. If you're travelling with two children, consider bringing a stroller board or a stroller sling.

You can bring your stroller or pram to both parks as long as it doesn't exceed the dimensions of 92 cm x 132 cm (remember to also follow your airline's sizes for checking through). Most airports allow access to the aeroplane gate, where they then remove it to place it in the hold. You should have it labelled and preferably in a cover or bag. Upon arrival at the airport, generally, it's collected at the baggage claim belt, like a checked suitcase, unless it's oversized, in which case it's collected at a separate counter.

If you're travelling alone with your baby, it's a good idea to bring a baby carrier or backpack, so you have both hands free for folding the pushchair. The best strollers for aeroplanes are the ones that fold to the size of a cabin suitcase, as when travelling with children, some airlines will allow you to keep it in the cabin, instead of having to put it in the hold, wait afterward, etc.

Once in the park, you're not allowed to take the strollers on attractions or into restaurants; and you must **park them in the designated area**. Although security problems are rare, don't leave anything valuable in them, and if your stroller is "tempting", a juicy latest model, also bring a lightweight lock. Try not to lock the stroller to any "Disney property" like benches or fences, but do block or join the wheels together. Another solution, if your stroller allows it, is to remove a wheel and keep it in your backpack.

Apart from identification, it's advisable to **customise** it so that it's easy to distinguish in the "sea of strollers". Coloured ribbons (or fluorescent sticks for the night) will make it impossible to miss and will delight the "passenger". If you have them, it's a good idea to use an AirTag to locate it more easily.

With unstable weather (not only during winter, as summer storms are very frequent in Paris), keep with you the **rain cover**, and secure it on the stroller when you ride on the attractions, to avoid finding it soaked on the way out. Don't forget the **sleeping bag** if you're travelling in winter. Even for cool summer nights, your children will appreciate a **fleece blanket.**

If your baby is small (or if you're also bringing another child), as we mentioned, it's advisable to also bring a **baby carrier backpack** or **sling wrap**. In several attractions (following the instructions of the Cast Members), you can get on directly with the baby in the backpack, without having to wake them up from naps, etc. If you are travelling with more children, having a carrier backpack will also allow them to take turns in the stroller.

Another option seen in the park are Bollerwagen carts, but unless you're carrying many children and bags, they're not recommended, as they manoeuvre poorly in crowded spaces.

Disneyland Paris offers **stroller rentals** for €30/day at "Roll-a-Long Rental" on Main Street, turning to the right after the park entrance, and at "Location Rentals" at the Studios. They're not the best option (unless by the second day you find them essential) for several reasons, besides the price: they're rigid and don't recline, and they don't offer much protection against rain.

Additionally, you have to pay a deposit of €50, or return them each day at the park exit, which could mean you end up carrying a child in your arms from that point to the hotel room or to the other park. If you use them, remember to personalise them as well, so you're not searching for yours name by name; and if possible, bring a small lock to prevent someone forgetful (or cheeky) from leaving you without it.

Cribs, High Chairs, and Other Baby Accessories

There are **baby changing tables** in virtually all restrooms in both parks and Disney Village. Of course, don't forget to bring a foldable changing mat, as waterproof as possible. You can find the nearest restroom in the park's App, at the interactive map. As said, almost all of them have baby changing facilities, and the quieter ones are those at the park's ends. During peak times, the central restrooms can have long lines, so it's better to head to ones like those at Toad Hall.

In the hotels, you can request a **folding crib** for the room when making the reservation or upon arrival (the mattress in some is very thinly padded, according to reports, due to French regulations). There are also bottle heaters available upon request (in some hotels with a deposit of €20), and even, depending on the hotel's availability, bottle sterilisers. Personally, I recommend MAM bottles, which self-sterilise in the microwave.

High chairs are available in all restaurants. You'll find high chairs in all restaurants (customised with Mickey, of course). In table-service restaurants, they can warm the baby's food for you, just ask the waiter; while in buffet-style and quick-service restaurants, there are microwaves to warm it yourselves.

It's most advisable to bring vacuum-packed jars, fruit pouches, etc. The journey is short but tiring, and it's preferable not to add unnecessary stress of figuring out how to prepare or preserve food. In Relay - Petit Monoprix points at the station and in some hotel shops, you can purchase yoghurt and juices. Another tip is to bring silicone or disposable bibs, to save space in the suitcase and not worry about laundry, as well as children's spoons and forks.

Although the rooms are child-friendly, another essential when travelling with babies is a roll of masking tape, which will help you turn any room into a safe and baby-proof space: you can cover sockets, prevent doors from closing or drawers from opening, and it leaves no marks when removed. Don't forget their pacifier, comforter, or night light either.

If you're travelling with a small baby, a crawling apron can come in very handy. You can also bring a travel picnic blanket, to give them space to move around, and for you to sit on during parade waits. On Amazon, they have mini picnic blankets, which, when spread out, measure just 70*110 cm and only 6*8 cm when folded. Prices start at €8.

Although it's not a common feature in a park designed to enjoy with children, there's also a babysitting service available at the hotels, upon request, for an extra fee.

Baby Care Centers

Baby Care Centers are dedicated places to care for your baby with a location in each Disney Park:

-   In Disneyland Park: on Main Street, U.S.A. turn right, next to the Plaza Gardens Restaurant

-   In Walt Disney Studios Park, behind Studio Services.

These centers have almost everything you need to look after your little ones: a feeding room with microwaves and high chairs, as well as child-sized toilets and changing tables (the latter are also available in most park restrooms, check with the App). The truth is that they're very much in need of an update (you can't access them with a stroller, which is illogical). They also lack a sink in the feeding area to wash baby bottles.

If needed, you can purchase some baby items in them: juices, baby food jars, pacifiers, sunscreen, etc. Keep in mind that something might be out of stock and that prices are "for emergencies", a pack of wipes costs about €6, a single diaper €1 or a pack for €20...

If you can't find what you want, or need a better price, head to the Relay at the station (next to the RER access). If you're looking for a pharmacy, the nearest one is next to Val d'Europe station, in the shopping center.

Breast-feeding area.

Although the park's breastfeeding policy allows mothers to feed their children anywhere the mother feels safe and comfortable, should they seek more privacy or need to use a breast pump with a plug, there are nursing rooms available. One located in Main Street, and another near the First Aid Center in the Studios, behind Studio Services.

Quiet Corners

If your baby needs a bit of tranquillity, for example, if they can't nap with noise; if you're on a high-affluence day and need to clear your head a bit, or if you're travelling with someone with special needs, high sensitivity, or ASD, there are other quiet corners hidden within the park, usually near attractions that are a bit secluded. Some of them can be found in the following lands:

In **Disneyland Park:**

- In **Fantasyland:** to the right of the "It's a Small World!" attraction, there's a quiet path that connects to Discoveryland, and that is often partially closed, as the afternoon parade comes out from this point.

- In **Adventureland:** near Temple Traders, in front of Indiana Jones.

- In **Frontierland:** next to the Lion King theatre.

- In **Discoveryland:** next to the theatre, behind Hyperspace Mountain.

In **Walt Disney Studios:**

- Next to Cars Road Trip, at the far end of the park, past the Toy Story land.

- Near the Super Diner restaurant, behind the Hollywood Tower of Terror.

For moments of unavoidable noise (parades, shows, etc.), both for babies and highly sensitive individuals, it's best to bring noise-cancelling headphones, which are quite common in parks.

Pregnancy

Disneyland Paris is a safe destination for pregnant women. Although there are attractions with restricted access, there are many other options as shows, quiet attractions, and character encounters for a fun day out, and the park team will strive to make the pregnant woman as comfortable as possible, providing special access to attractions and shows.

To do this, you must present an original medical certificate at the ticket booths (Donald Desk), signed and stamped by the doctor, and must not be older than 3 months. It must state the pregnancy and personal details in English or French. With this step, you will be issued a priority access bracelet (Bracelet Panpan). Along with this bracelet, you will receive the **Special Access Card** for Pregnant Women, a nominative card that includes your information and those of your companions.

This card, which does not entitle you to discounts on tickets, functions as a **booklet for a virtual queue**. You only need to show it to the Cast Member at the entrance of the chosen attraction, and they will give you a time slot for you and up to 4 companions to enjoy the attraction again, skipping the queue. Once you have enjoyed that attraction, they will mark it off the card, and you can proceed to another (or even the same one) and fill out a new "virtual queue" in the booklet.

Likewise, by showing this card, you will have access to a priority area for **parades**, this time accompanied by only 2 people, although if they are children, Cast Members usually allow more companions. **Stores,** (which are full of new born items!), also have a priority checkout counter, where you can pay without waiting in line by asking the nearest Cast Member.

Remember to bring snacks, crackers, etc. Prices for snacks in the park are high, and queues can be unbearable when you have a craving. Of course, don't forget any prescribed medication, especially if you have nausea or hyperemesis, as fatigue and heavier meals increase dizziness.

In general, the food is suitable for pregnant women, except for some exceptions. You can consult with Cast Members for any details, such as whether the cheese is pasteurised, if any recipe contains pâtés, or request that the meat be cooked a little more; they will be happy to assist upon hearing "Je suis enceinte".

In our "Lands and Attractions" table, you can see which attractions you can enjoy without restrictions. Should you have any doubts, check the Cast Members about that specific experience.

Disability and Priority Card

People with disabilities are welcome at Disneyland Paris, where Cast Members and the rest of the team will strive to make their visit as comfortable as possible. As for which attractions you can enjoy, there are many options available. Disneyland offers, on its website, as part of its MagicALL initiative, Accessibility Plans, with information about each attraction: whether there are steps, the availability for sign language interpreters, strobe lights, etc.

They also provide information regarding wheelchair access, whether you can directly access the attraction vehicle in the wheelchair or if you need to transfer from the wheelchair to the wagon within a limited time.

There is also a small guide ("The Blue Booklet"), which can be downloaded from the park's website, containing tips for visiting Disneyland Paris for people with autism spectrum disorders, ADHD, and non-neurotypical individuals.

In these cases, it is advisable to know our "Quiet Corners", which you will find in the "Travelling with Babies" section, and bring noise-cancelling headphones or earplugs, as well as familiar objects, as the hustle and bustle and sounds of the park can be overwhelming at certain times.

For people with visual impairments, the AudioSpot app provides an audio description system for the scenes of the attractions in English or French; and, in the case of restaurants, the menu is detailed in 9 languages.

Holders of disability certificates, and their companions, are entitled to a 25% discount on 1-day / 1-park and 1-day / 2-park tickets purchased at the ticket booth, as well as a 25% discount on the Disneyland Pass when purchased at the ticket booth. To do this, they must present a document proving the disability. A medical certificate is not valid; it must be an official document; check Disneyland Paris's website for the documents listed for your country, although in general, any of the following are considered valid:

- Disability Degree Certificate
- Disability Accreditation Card
- Parking Card

If visitors have an Annual Pass or undated ticket, they must register the visit date in advance on the park's website. However, this is not necessary if they purchase a ticket on the same day of the visit at the ticket booth, showing the certificate. There is no "quota" of tickets available at the ticket booth, so if you go on a busy day when the park is full, you will have to purchase it for another date.

When purchasing the ticket, you will be asked to fill out a questionnaire with some questions about autonomy and safety, and you will be given a **Priority Card** with your photo. Depending on the degree of autonomy, the possibility of evacuation, the need for assistance, etc. The card will have a distinctive colour, ranging from Green (autonomous, no mobility issues) to Grey.

To save time, the Priority Card can also be requested in advance, from one month before your visit. By doing this, you only have to show the document proving the disability at the ticket office, purchase the ticket, and you will be given the Priority Card that you had previously requested.

https://www.disneylandparis.com/en-gb/guest-services/priority-card/

With this card, the disabled person and their companions (the number may vary, but in the attractions, they can admit up to 4 companions) will have priority access or priority attention in attractions, reserved space to watch the shows, character encounters, restaurants, shops, and receptions. Remember to carry a wide lanyard where the card fits, as you will need to show it at all these access points. The Cast Member will indicate where to access, typically through the exit of the attraction or through a special entrance.

This priority access does not mean immediate access, but sometimes you will be given a ticket with an assigned time slot, allowing you to visit other attractions or shows in the meantime. For the Princess Pavilion or other character encounters, it is advisable to request priority access tickets in the morning, as they easily run out.

The person with a disability, along with a single companion (although if there are children in the group, they will normally be allowed) can watch the parades from a reserved area, in the Town Square part. Similarly, for the night-time show, there is another reserved area, on the left side of the square, next to the entrance to Adventureland.

All restaurants and toilets in the park offer adapted toilets for people with disabilities. Likewise, adapted rooms are available at all Disney hotels, with extra space for wheelchair access and adapted bathrooms. To reserve them, you just have to call the reservation number, by phone, or through Skype.

There are also reserved parking spots both at the park and at all Disney Hotels, located the closest to the entrance.

Access with standard wheelchairs, electric wheelchairs, and vehicles adapted for people with reduced mobility is allowed. You can check the requirements for the latter in the park regulations available on the website.

Finally, if you suffer an injury and need a wheelchair, you can rent them at the Stroller/Pushchair and Wheelchair Rental shop (Roll-a-Long Rental), located at Disneyland® Park by the entrance at Town Square Terrace, and at Location Rentals, placed at Walt Disney Studios® Park near Studio Services.

The price is about €25/day, and for an extra deposit of €200, you can take them out of the park to your hotel. The rental chairs are quite basic. If what you need is an electric option, or a mobility scooter, there are rental companies that provide this service, such as Mobility Equipment, but it is required to book it in advance.

https://www.mobilityequipmenthiredirect.com/

Long-term Illness or Long-term Chronic Disease

Disneyland offers an easy access card for people with a **long-term illness (LTI)** or long-term chronic disease. On the park's website, you can check the list of diseases included in this status, it includes a wide range of situations, from diabetes to heart diseases.

To obtain the card, a medical certificate in French or English must be presented, certifying the illness included in the list. The certificate must not be older than 3 months.

This card allows quick access (although not immediate) to attractions and shows. You just have to show it to the nearest Cast Member, who will give you a ticket with an appointment, to access at a specific time slot without waiting.

If you suffer from a temporary health problem, such as a sprain or similar, try to request the facilitated access card, providing a medical certificate less than three months old, in English or French. Although it is not a general rule, they may give you priority access exceptionally, and at the discretion of Disneyland Paris.

Storage of Special Medicines

At Disneyland Paris, there are a few spots where you can store medication that needs to be kept cool. Special products must be packaged (in a plastic bag, airtight container, box, icebox...), sealed, and clearly labelled with the guest's name (using an adhesive label or permanent markers). No other medical equipment can be held by Disneyland Paris, but in this case, you can also get in touch with outside companies through the Central Reservation Office

You can deposit medications at the following locations:

- In the **Disney Parks**: at one of the First Aid Posts:

    - In **Disneyland Park**: between Discovery Arcade and Plaza Gardens Restaurant, on Main Street, U.S.A.

    - In **Walt Disney Studios,** between Studio Services and Studio Photo, in the Front Lot.

- In **Disney Village**: at the First Aid Post.

- In the **Hotels:** at Reception at Disney hotels, and Hôtel l'Élysée Val d'Europe and in the refrigerators available at the bungalows at Davy Crockett Ranch and Villages Nature Paris. Keep in mind that this kind of medical product should not be kept in the minibar fridge of a regular hotel room.

Once more, bear in mind the importance of travelling with the corresponding medical prescription, to avoid problems at security checks. For convenience, more and more families choose to carry a mini-electric fridge, which can be charged to any socket in the room. There are models on the market with dimensions smaller than 22 x 10 x 10 cm, which will guarantee you a stable temperature and immediate access to medication.

First Aid and Emergencies

It is normal for your day at the park to go smoothly without any incidents, but in case you need medical assistance, it is advisable to know the locations of the First Aid Points, which you can also locate through the App.

- In **Disneyland Park**: between Discovery Arcade and Plaza Gardens Restaurant, at the end of Main Street USA, to the right

- In **Walt Disney Studios**, between Studio Services and Studio Photo, in the Front Lot.

In addition, both Disney Village and the hotels have their own First Aid Points. All of them have personnel trained for medical emergencies (with millions of visitors each year, they are accustomed to any problem that may arise) but they can also help with small unforeseen events, such as needing a pain killer, band-aids, or any other pharmacy item.

If you hold one, remember to bring your European Health Insurance Card (EHIC) or UK Global Health Insurance Card (GHIC), in case you need specialised medical attention. It is also advisable to complement it with Travel Insurance, as the French public health system requires co-payment.

In the event of a cardiac arrest, AED's (automated external defibrillators) are installed throughout the park. These are medical devices that measure heart rate and operate autonomously to send an electric pulse to the heart if necessary (Cast Members are trained to use them, and the device itself provides step-by-step verbal instructions so that any guest can operate it without training). All AED's deployed at Disneyland Paris are suitable for use on adults and children. You will find them next to most toilet areas, and you can see their location on the map of the App.

In case of an accident or serious emergency, these are the telephone numbers of the French emergency services:

Emergency— 112
Ambulances — 15 or 112
Police — 17 or 112
Fire Brigade— 18 or 112
24-hour Health Care— 01 47 07 77 77

Pharmacies and Pharmacy Items

If the First Aid Point does not have what you need, you can go to the nearest pharmacy. This is located in the Val d'Europe shopping center, at the entrance to Place d'Ariane, next to the train station. It is open every day. To get to Val d'Europe, you can take the RER (suburban train), just one stop from the park station. You can also take the free bus line No. 50, or a taxi in front of the station, for about €5 per trip. At the Auchan hypermarket in the shopping center, pharmacy items can also be found, such as band-aids or analgesics, as well as at the minimarket at Marne - La Vallée - Chessy station.

Travelling with Elderly People

Throughout this guide, we have focused mostly on children, of course, but on many occasions, the trip includes older people. As we mentioned, Disneyland Paris has attractions for all tastes, and the elderly will enjoy many of them, as well as finding classic settings, such as the old-fashioned Dapper Dan's Hair Cut barbershop (where you can even book a haircut or shave), the steamboat of Thunder Mesa Riverboat Landing, the vintage cars of Main Street Vehicles or the retro futuristic style of Autopia.

Some ailments associated with age, such as heart diseases or diabetes, are included in the list of Long-term Illnesses, and you can get the facilitated access LTI card for them.

Access to certain attractions is restricted for visitors with cervical or back problems; however, there are many quiet rides and leisure strolls available for those in this situation.

It is advisable to bring a folding bench to make waits in attractions or shows more bearable. Additionally, if walking long distances becomes challenging, the Disneyland Railroad steam locomotive connects different areas of Disneyland Park.

Guide Dogs, Assistance Animals, and Pets

Access to the parks with assistance dogs, or guide dogs for blind or visually impaired people, is allowed. They must be kept on a leash at all times and be under the owner's control. For this, a medical certificate may be required, the animal should be fully vaccinated, and their access is limited to some attractions (you can check in the Assistance Animals section and the accessibility plan available online).

Access is also allowed with emotional support animals (only dogs or cats) to the parks, as long as a medical certificate is presented specifying the need, they are fully vaccinated and kept on a leash at all times, and are under the owner's control.

Again, their access is limited to some attractions (it is advisable to check the accessibility plan). If the support animal is a dog, it must not belong to the category of dangerous dogs in French regulations.

If you travel with cats or dogs outside of these medical reasons, they can stay, for an additional fee (roughly €25 per day and €25 per night, food and water are included in the price), at the Pet Center located next to the visitor parking lot. The cast will take care of your animal, but you're responsible to take it for a walk if needed. Your animal must be microchipped and have an up-to-date rabies vaccination certificate (more than a month and less than one-year-old) translated into French and issued by an official vet. In this case, breeds classified as "dangerous" in French regulations cannot access either.

The capacity of the Center is limited and cannot be reserved in advance; once it reaches its full capacity, your pet will not be admitted. Always consider a plan B if you travel during peak times. Some rooms at Davy Crockett Ranch also allow dogs, as we mentioned, at a cost of €30/day and under certain conditions that you can check on the website and by phone.

Long Lasting Magic

Throughout these pages, we've covered all the essential aspects of the trip. However, if you want to capture the best photos, discover more features of the park's architecture, or if you're celebrating a special occasion, like a birthday, don't miss the following tips to extend your magic experience even further.

The Best Photos of Your Trip

Disneyland is a unique journey to enjoy with your loved ones, filled with great moments and memories that you'll certainly want to capture. Some visitors carry close-to-professional equipment, but it's only recommended if that's your main interest. Such cameras require constant attention and care from you, to avoid any damage during rides, or exposure in the rain, and it will be another valuable item to keep an eye on all the time. With a good phone, you'll have fantastic photos and fewer worries.

Another fun option, if you're very interested in meeting and engaging with characters, is instant cameras. These allow you to take a photo and ask the character for their signature, adding a touch of celebrity glamour. Many children carry kids' cameras (available on Amazon, for about 20 euros, memory card sold separately); the photo quality won't be the best, but they'll treasure those memories captured from their own perspective.

If you want high-quality photos, or ones taken on rides, you can buy them on the Photopass website or hire the Photopass+ service.

Photopass

This is Disney's system to access photos taken by professional photographers and on-ride photos of attractions. When the photo is taken, the photographer will hand you a card to access the Photopass website, where you can view the photo and purchase it for download if you wish. There are two locations in the park ("New Century Notions" in Main Street and "Walt Disney Studios Store" in the Studios), where you can even print them instantly. Each photo costs between 14 and 19 €, and is available for purchase on the website for 1 year.

https://www.disneyphotopass.eu/

There are six attractions that take "On-Ride" photos during the experience: in Disneyland Park: Big Thunder Mountain, Pirates of the Caribbean, on the second drop, Buzz Lightyear, and HyperSpace Mountain; and in Walt Disney Studios: Avengers Assemble: Flight Force and Tower of Terror, when the elevator door opens at the top of the tower.

Photopass+ and Photopass+ Premium

Photopass+: This service allows you to access all photos taken by professional photographers, costing 75 €, and allows for unlimited download of all your photos, at no additional cost. It is purchased during booking or at the park itself, and the price is valid for all people included in the booking (not per person, but per booking).

Once you obtain the Photopass+ card, just simply show it to the photographer and he will associate the photos with your account, to ensure they are correctly saved on your card. For "On-Ride" photos, at the exit of the attraction, you will find a Photopass booth. There you can link the photo code to your Photopass+ card and it will become available on the website for download. The card can be used for 10 days from the first activation, and the photos are available for a year. In the event of losing the physical card, it can be recovered with the purchase code.

Photopass+ Premium: this package is exclusively available for purchase at the Avengers Campus stores. Priced at 90€, it includes all the features from the Photopass+ version and all the recordings with characters at the Hero Training Center, in the Avengers Campus. The videos can also be purchased separately, opting for this service is only worthwhile if you want to acquire many of them.

Nevertheless, if you simply want a nice family picture, there is no need to purchase Photopass or Photopass+, just politely ask a Cast Member if they can take a photo with your camera or phone; they are very skilled and do a great job. Remember that selfie sticks are not permitted in the park for safety reasons.

Magic Shots

The "Magic Shots" photographers take photos with effects, similar to Instagram filters. These can include characters, balloons, rainbows, or decorations related to special holidays like Halloween or Christmas. All photos are available at Photopass, for purchase, or to download if you have Photopass+ contracted. You'll see them throughout the park and their locations are also on the App.

The Best Locations for Your Photos

Throughout the park, there are countless spots to take beautiful photos; let's not forget that it's a great fairy tale setting. We're going to tell you about our favourite and less crowded locations to get the perfect snapshot.

Sleeping Beauty Castle: it's the main focal point of the park and a special memory of your trip, although it's usually very crowded. We advise you to try during Extra Magic Time, or by accessing at 8:15 if you book the first turn of Character Breakfast at Plaza Gardens restaurant.

Outside of that time, if you want to improve the photo with fewer "extras" passing by, go to the left side of the Castle, there you have three points from which to take photos with fewer people:

- The first, and closest to the Castle, is just to the left of it, you will find a small balcony, play with the angles and the Castle's railing will cover part of the visitors entering by the bridge!

- The second, a bit further left, is the bridge that serves as the entrance to the Dragon's Lair (don't forget to visit it while you're there).

- And the third and farthest is the path that connects Adventureland with Fantasyland, leading from the Agrabah area to the Seven Dwarfs shop. From there, the Castle is surrounded by trees and "square" hedges following the original settings of the Sleeping Beauty movie.

On the other hand, another beautiful and less crowded perspective for a photo with the Castle in the background is on the other side, in Fantasyland, in front of Cinderella's statue at Auberge. There you'll find a pink corner with flowers, and the Castle will be in the background to the right.

Finally, if your kids are not tired, you can try from the Castle theatre at sunset, when the light is prettier, or at night, after the fireworks. The Castle is lit in pink and the shops are open for an hour after the park's official closing, so you can get that magical photo with the Castle almost empty.

A good trick to make the Castle stand out more in the photo on our phone is to get closer to the person being photographed, and slowly zoom in on the Castle on the screen while walking slowly backward. In many terminals, the phone's camera will recognize the point of interest and enhance it.

After the Castle, perhaps the most iconic photo in the park is **with your favourite character.** As we mentioned in the "Costumes" section, an added bonus in children's character meetings is to go dressed as their favourite character, their archenemy, or their pet; the characters know their role perfectly and interactions are usually very fun!

Cinderella's carriage: located outside Auberge de Cendrillon, will delight fans of fairy tales. Don't forget to pay a visit to Snow White's wishing well, on the right side of the Castle.

The horses of **Lancelot's Carousel** are the setting for very endearing photos. Next to the Carousel, on a pedestal, you'll see King Arthur's Sword, Excalibur itself. Try to pull it out, just in case the King of England is among you! At night, with few people and the Castle lit up in the background, the photo is magical.

The **Alice's Curious Labyrinth** area is another fun spot for photos, where you'll find the Queen's throne, the unbirthday tea table, or the card-soldiers inside the maze, in the middle of a rose-painting session.

The classic **Mad Hatter's Tea Cups** attraction is a great photo spot, although you may need your best photography skills, both playing with motion and at night, when the ceiling lanterns are lit. Don't worry if they come out very blurry, there's a "loose" cup outside that's fool proof!

The **Agrabah** area is presided over by Aladdin's lamp, from which mysterious smoke emerges... is the Genie in the sauna? Rub the lamp and ask him for a wish! At the Pirate Galleon and Skull Rock, the best photos are taken next to Captain Hook's Meet and Greet spot, hopefully with the Captain himself!

The **Pink Porch,** a very pretty balustrade on Main Street, with a facade of the same colour and the Coca-Cola truck located opposite, are perfect for the most "retro" photos for your Instagram.

If, after all you've seen, your kids dream of being part of the park's cast, look for the "casting door" on Main Street (entering, on the left, the facade is orange) and take a photo of them "submitting resumes" in front of Walt Disney's quote, "It Takes People to Make the Dream a Reality".

As for **Walt Disney Studios,** it's full of places to take good photos, such as the spectacular surroundings of the Avenger Campus, or Toy Story Playland. In this latter land, you'll see several photocalls, like the parachutes, or two Backstage doors painted with Buzz Lightyear's wings and the "The Claw" moment next to Cars Road Trip. Don't miss Buzz's talking statue, or Rex in the midst of a nervous breakdown.

Next to Crush's Coaster, you'll find an area dedicated to Monsters, Inc. with Boo's door and a "scream-o-meter". The Flying Carpets over Agrabah attraction features a small balcony, in case you want to take photos of your group on its magic carpet.

These are some spots but there are a thousand more. Be creative, improvise, and take advantage of your children's surprise reactions and the small details; that photo with Mickey's ice creams, or your baby with a balloon and the Castle in the background will become your favourite wallpaper. Also, look for hidden corners, like the Arcades at night. In many cases, the trick is to play with perspective or park elements, as the attractions' photocalls, "high-fiving" the statue of Walt Disney, or "inside the buckets" of the Fantasia broom that carries water to its fountain.

Celebrating a Birthday

A trip to Disneyland Paris can be the ultimate birthday gift. If you also want to celebrate it with a special touch, you can order a birthday cake at any table-service restaurant. You will be served a chocolate cake decorated with Mickey, and candles or sparklers; it's quite generous (serves 8 people) and costs €35. You can add it when making a reservation at the restaurant or purchase it at the checkout on the same day; it doesn't have to be the exact day of the birthday. Usually, Cast Members bring it out lit, singing "Happy Birthday." But if it's at a character dining restaurant and coincides, a character may come to join you at that moment.

Don't forget to pick up your free celebration button at City Hall, Studio Services, or the Disney hotels' reception. You'll have Cast Members wishing you a happy birthday throughout the day, and perhaps some special surprises!

Also, at City Hall and Studio Services, and at some receptions (such as the breakfasts at the Newport hotel), they can arrange for the child to receive "a call" from Mickey Mouse himself, wishing them a happy birthday, a touching and free memory.

As mentioned in the "Costumes" section, for those with more generous budgets, the Disneyland Hotel offers the "My Royal Dream" service, which turns the child into a prince or princess for a day. There are also face-painting stations in Fantasyland.

You can also book extra surprises through dlp.disney.special.activities@disney.com, such as gifts in the room or personalised guides. These surprises are VIP-level, and accordingly priced. If you prefer to allocate the budget to other expenses, still mention it at check-in or send an email to the hotel reception; sometimes they leave a little something in the room "from Mickey". You can even let Cast Members or store staff know, as in some stores, such as the Lego Store, they sometimes offer a special 15% birthday discount or a small gift.

Other Curiosities and Experiences in the Park

The Disney park's "Imagineers", the team of engineers, architects, decorators, and illustrators who bring magic to life, are the world's leaders in creating amusement parks. Thanks to them, Disneyland Paris is perhaps one of the most beautiful and well-kept parks in the world.

They are specialists not only in creating magic and details visible to visitors but also in hiding necessary but less aesthetic things. Therefore, in all Disney parks, there is a network of tunnels, a veritable underground world colour-coded through which Cast Members and characters circulate.

The park's architecture is meticulously crafted, with a play of perspectives to make the Castle look impressive without exceeding France's height restrictions, which would require aviation lights for safety. Furthermore, the technical facilities that are on the surface are painted a special colour, the "disappearing green", which makes the eye overlook them and focus on everything else.

If you're eager to learn more about the park's construction, there is a **guided tour** available in English, French, and Spanish, where you'll learn about the history, architecture, and best-kept secrets of Disneyland Paris. It can be booked at City Hall in Disneyland Park or at the Studio Services in the Studios, for an extra fee, which does not include priority access to attractions or shows.

Another little-known experience in the park, but sought after by regular visitors and experts, is the **guided botanical route.** Disneyland Paris is Europe's largest garden, with over 450 plant species and thousands of trees, and some unique specimens.

The guided tours ("Nature Trails") focus on its biodiversity, with routes through the Cheyenne hotel (where you'll see the rose garden and the nearby orchard that supplies the hotel's restaurant); or the bee garden and the forests of Davy Crockett Ranch. Moreover, during the visit, you can learn more about the park's flora through the official app.

After the Trip

Your visit to Disneyland Paris has ended, but the magic hasn't! Throughout this chapter, we'll give you ideas to complete the experience back home, and, of course, all the secrets to extend your trip visiting the French capital with your children.

Visiting Paris with Kids

Taking advantage of your trip to Disneyland to explore Paris is a fantastic idea. In these pages, we'll show you the most emblematic and iconic places for a family getaway to the French capital.

Furthermore, if the park is just one stage of a longer trip around France, soon you'll have available our guide **"Travelling with Kids to Paris"**, with all the secrets to enjoy the city with children, the most appealing plans in central Paris, and the best destinations in the surrounding areas, including Parc Astérix.

A handy tip is to mark these places on a **Google Maps map**. Whether they're part of your main itinerary or you fancy getting lost in the streets of Paris, you'll always know what activities and places are nearby.

Go City Card (Paris Pass)

The Paris tourist card, "Go City", formerly known as the "Paris Pass", allows you to visit several attractions for a flat fee and access priority lines at several of them, such as the Louvre, the Musée d'Orsay, or the Palace of Versailles.

Prices vary depending on the days chosen and whether you opt for the All-Inclusive Pass or the Explorer Pass. Passes of 4 days or more include a card, the Museum Pass, providing access to over 60 museums. It's advisable to book it on the official website, which offers refunds in case of cancellation (allowing you to buy with confidence, knowing that you can get a refund if your plans change unexpectedly) and occasional discount codes.

www.gocity.com/paris
www.parispass.com

The card is cost-effective if your goal is to thoroughly explore Paris and its museums. If you only want to take a stroll, do a tour on the tourist bus, and visit the Eiffel Tower, it's worth booking each plan separately.

Other alternatives include websites like Civitatis, where you can book passes, tickets, and experiences together. If your budget is tight, in Civitatis, you'll find free tours that, for a symbolic price, will show you all the city's secrets.

Take the opportunity to practise the language, adults and children alike! There are many apps to refresh your French, such as **Babbel** or **Duolingo**, and free versions like **Très bien**.

Transports and Tourist Bus

If you visit Paris after several days in the park, your children may be a little tired of walking, and distances in Paris are considerable. One solution is to book a Tourist Bus, which will take you "door to door" to each monument. You can hop on and off whenever you want, saving yourselves walks and transfers.

It's a great option in many cases: if you have little time, if you're travelling with babies (the metro is full of complicated staircases for strollers), or simply for the convenience of seeing everything from the double-decker bus (in the front row on the second floor, you'll be covered and have more space for backpacks and a stroller).

There are several companies offering this service, with different stops, schedules, and fares. The most well-known is **Big Bus Paris**, which is also included in the Go City card. In this case, it's usually worthwhile to book the card, with the bus and the visit to the Eiffel Tower included, and they provide an audio guide.

Both the tourist bus and regular buses are good options to explore Paris comfortably, although not the only ones. The **metro** network is extensive and covers the whole city, although it's not very accessible due to stairs, making it difficult for those with very young children. On the other hand, services like **Welcome, Uber,** or **Taxi G7** will allow you to add boosters or child seats to your transportation reservation.

Travelling with Babies to Paris

If you're travelling with babies, take the most collapsible and compact stroller possible, as Paris is not the most accessible city for them, and part of its charm lies in small cafes, corners, and stairways (especially in the Latin Quarter and Montmartre). It's also advisable to bring a baby carrier for the metro and to access monuments where strollers aren't allowed.

The toilets, in general, don't have changing tables, except in museums or department stores (pay attention to Ikea stores, especially the one on Rivoli Street). There's also an extensive network of public toilets that will save you in case of emergency. In addition to the travel changer (preferably waterproof), it's a good idea to bring along a disposable one or a changing pad, in case that a changing space is hard to find.

There are also portable high chairs available in the form of briefcases, which not only store food but also serve as a convenient solution for dining in Parisian restaurants, which typically don't provide them.

What to visit in Paris

Paris is an incredibly beautiful city...and a vast one! This is especially true when exploring it with children. In this section, we will focus on the best monuments, museums, and parks to visit Paris as a family, as well as where to grab a bite or find a small souvenir or toy from the French capital.

Eiffel Tower

The Eiffel Tower is the heart of France and its most recognizable symbol. You can't leave Paris without experiencing the view from the top and enjoying the views of the entire city. It's open every day of the year with extended hours, but since it's the most visited monument in the world, it's crucial to book tickets in advance on the Tower's website (otherwise, the wait in line can exceed 2 hours).

On certain dates like Christmas, Valentine's Day, or Easter, tickets sell out quickly. If you have the Go City card (Paris Pass), which includes a visit to the Eiffel Tower, you still need to book the date and time on the official website:

www.toureiffel.paris/en

If you've run out of tickets and lack flexibility with dates, consider purchasing them through Civitatis or book a Paris Pass tour for an extra fee.

The Tower offers three levels of observation decks: the first floor at 57m high, the second at 115m, and the summit at 276 metres. Ticket prices start at €11.30 for adults and vary depending on the observation deck you want to access and whether you choose to climb the stairs (almost 700 steps) or take the elevator to the second floor. Additionally, there are reduced rates for children, youth, and disabled individuals, while children under 4 years old can access for free.

To enter, you must pass through two security checkpoints: at the entrance of the premises and just before going up the Tower through a pillar. Do not bring any objects that could be considered dangerous, nor excessively large suitcases (there are no lockers in the Tower).

Electronic tickets are nominative, and you must bring your identity documents, including those of the children. At the time indicated on your electronic ticket, you must be at the "Visitors with tickets" entrance. It is recommended to arrive 15 minutes early to go through security checks.

Once at the Tower, it's best to go directly to the top observation deck and then work your way down. You can bring a stroller for babies, although you'll have to fold it to enter the elevators, since space on the observation decks is limited. There are baby changing tables in the restrooms on all floors except the summit, and access to them is free.

The Eiffel Tower offers a free visitor guide that you can access on your mobile phone. Free Wi-Fi network (_WiFi_Tour_Eiffel) is available to all visitors.

Situated between the Tower and the river, there's a beautiful classic two-story carousel, a must if you're accompanied by very young children—they'll love it! Moreover, if your visit coincides with July 14th, the French National Day, don't miss the fireworks from the Champ de Mars, which turn the Eiffel Tower into the star of the light and colour show.

Notre Dame Cathedral

During your stroll through Paris, you can't miss the magnificent Notre Dame Cathedral, the home of the famous Quasimodo. Unfortunately, following the fire it suffered in 2019, it is currently closed for restoration works, and interior visits are suspended. Its reopening is expected on December 8, 2024. Nevertheless, the exterior of the cathedral is magnificent, and you can still enjoy the views of its towers and gargoyles from the surroundings or aboard a boat sailing on the Seine.

Seine River Cruise

Cruising along the Seine by boat is one of the most beautiful routes Paris has to offer. Moreover, it's a fantastic plan with young children, sparing them from long walks, while it also provides them with the thrill of sailing beneath the city's iconic bridges. Try not to bring a baby stroller as there are long flights of stairs to access decks.

Seeing the city from the water provides a unique and close perspective of the incredible Parisian architecture, as both riverbanks are quite close. Even while Notre Dame is closed, it's the closest way to see the cathedral. Keep an eye out for the Île de la Cité; you might catch a marriage proposal—don't forget to applaud!

While this activity is included in the Paris Pass card, you also have the option to book it separately. Several companies offer approximately one-hour cruises: **Bateaux Parisiens, Batobus** (with hop-on-hop-off service, like tourist buses), or the most important and economical, **Bateaux Mouches.**

The rates for the latter are very competitive, especially for children: €15 for adults, €6 for children under 13, and free for children under 4. You can purchase tickets online through their website, where you can also see the schedules from the Alma Bridge or even book meals or picnics on board.

www.bateaux-mouches.fr/en/reservation/tickets

Parks and Paris Plages

Paris boasts countless large parks with plenty of options for children's activities, such as **Parc Rives-de-Seine**, **Jardins de Nelson Mandela,** or **Jardins de Luxembourg** (home to a classic puppet theatre), as well as hidden green corners like **Square du Vert-Galant.**

The Jardin des Tuileries is perhaps the most emblematic park in Paris. Walking through it, you'll reach from the Louvre to the Champs-Élysées, crossing the Place de la Concorde with its obelisk. Since 1850, between April and November, one of the classic traditions for Parisian children is sailing scale model boats on the Grand Basin of the Tuileries. They can choose a boat from the fleet (inspired by traditional French boats) and navigate it across the pond with a long pole, for a price of about €4.

www.les-petits-bateaux.fr

Near the entrance of Castiglione, there's a free-access children's area and a beautiful hand-painted classic carousel (€3 per ride). Furthermore, near the Grand Couvert, there's a rope bridge; and, to the north of the gardens, next to the monument to Puss in Boots, there are trampolines for children over 2 years old, which they'll love (€3).

If you have the time, you can extend your visit to the suburban parks of Paris. From **Parc Manceau**, which offers pony rides on holidays and a small classic carousel, to the **Bois de Boulogne,** with its classic amusement park Jardin d'Acclimatation, there's plenty to explore.

Additionally, the **Botanical Garden of Plants** is filled with activities for children, from the **Museum of Natural History** to the interactive exhibition of the **Galerie des Enfants.**

Lastly, during the summer months, in July and August, the right bank of the Seine and the pools of the Villette Basin become **Paris Plages,** or river beaches, featuring swimming pools, sun loungers, umbrellas, and a myriad of family-friendly and sports activities. In 2024, these activities will be affected by the celebration of the **Olympic Games,** with sports events taking place on the Seine.

Museums to visit with children

Paris is the city of great museums, but also of small galleries and curiosity museums; many of them organise activities for children or are especially interesting for them. If you have the time, it's worth getting the Museum Pass in addition to the Go City card; furthermore, some museums are accessible for free on the first Sunday of each month, such as the **Centre Pompidou** and the **Musée d'Orsay.**

The Louvre Museum

Visiting France's most important museum is an investment in culture that you should plan ahead for (as the shortest route takes a little over two hours). It's advisable to buy the ticket online, costing €17, and European children and youth enter for free up to 26 years old. Although it's included in the Museum Pass / Go City, you also need to reserve the day of the visit in advance on the official Louvre website:

www.louvre.fr/en/visit

Avoid the Pyramid entrance (especially if you already purchased the Go City card), although spectacular, it's always crowded! It's better to access through the lesser-known entrances, such as the Richelieu Passage, the Lion's Gate, and the Carousel Gallery.

A visit to the Louvre isn't complete without seeing its iconic masterpiece, the Mona Lisa. Leonardo da Vinci's small portrait of La Gioconda was painted with a unique technique, which creates the illusion that the lady's gaze follows you from any angle in the room. Additionally, her enigmatic smile seems to appear and disappear depending on where you stand.

Other masterpieces at the Louvre include Liberty Leading the People, by Delacroix, a symbol of the French Revolution, and The Raft of the Medusa, by Géricault.

Children will love the collection of Egyptian art, as famous as it is contested; at home, you can watch the film "Asterix and Cleopatra" to fully immerse yourselves. Speaking of movies, don't miss seeing Venus de Milo as she featured in the Hercules movie!

In the Richelieu wing, on the lower floor, below the grand Pyramid, there's a space dedicated for young visitors called The Studio. Here, children can participate in free art-related activities specifically designed for them, conducted in French. Additionally, The Studio provides a room with changing tables, high chairs, a microwave, and a nursing chair for added convenience.

Restrooms are available in the reception area under the Pyramid and in the galleries, and most of them are equipped with baby changing tables. You can access the museum with a baby stroller, although if it's too large, it won't fit in the elevators.

In any case, at the assistance counter under the Pyramid, you can borrow strollers for free by depositing an identity document. Additionally, you have the option to rent a Nintendo DS that serves as an audio guide for about €5.

Other Museums in Paris

If you have a little more time, there are countless museums to explore in Paris. After the Louvre, the **Musee d'Orsay** and the **Musee de l'Orangerie** are the most important, together housing the world's largest collection of Impressionist paintings. They also offer various family activities, guided tours, and art-related games. If you prefer your children to experience some modern art, you can visit the **Centre Pompidou** or the **Musée en Herbe,** a contemporary gallery with nods to pop culture.

Little researchers will enjoy the **City of Children,** within the City of Science and Industry, and **Science Experiences,** an interactive museum full of immersive experiences. Additionally, Paris is home to other small, curious, and lesser-known museums, such as the **Museum of Magic**, the **Fairground Arts Museum,** or the **Museum of Arts and Crafts**. And why not visit **The Chocolate Gourmet Museum** as well?

Restaurants and Cafés for Families

Paris is full of incredible restaurants, some are very romantic, delighting guests with exquisite dishes. However, iit can be a bit challenging to navigate them with children and strollers. If you're a small group with older children, you can try classic Parisian places like **Chez Janou, Sacrée Fleur, Le Cinq** or **L'Ange 20**, but perhaps you prefer options that are a bit more spacious, stress-free, and offer simple food for all tastes.

An easy idea to try with children is typical creperies, such as **Midi 12**, near Galeries Lafayette, **Lucette fait des Crêpes**, near Saint-Lazare, or **La Crêpe Rit du Clown**, located on the Left Bank, as well as **Les Freres Bretons**, near the Eiffel Tower.

Family lunch at **Hotel Chouchou** or the gastronomic proposals of **Valma, PIC/NIC**, or **L'Entrecote de Paris** will delight all palates. Furthermore, several of these restaurants feature "kid-friendly" spaces or entertainers to keep the little ones busy. Another great plan is to have lunch or dinner while cruising the Seine aboard the **Bateau le Calife**.

If your children find it hard to sit in a restaurant, the stalls at **Les Enfants Rouges** market or the **Monge Market** are a great solution. Here you can try different food options or take them away: from typical cheeses and French specialties to Asian, Italian, vegan and more, catering for all tastes!

Additionally, Paris is full of bakeries and pastry shops where you can try baguettes, croissants, and pains au chocolat. From the oldest ones like the nearly century-old **Poilâne** or **La Flûte Gana**, to more modern chains like **Maison Kayser.**

Shopping in Paris

A shopping tour in Paris will leave you amazed, particularly if you're seeking clothes or toys for the children. After all, France is the birthplace of renowned children's fashion brands like Bonpoint, Petit Bateau, Jacadi, or Cyrillus, along with charming toys from Moulin Roty or Vilac. Moreover, Paris is home to grand shopping arcades like **Galeries Lafayette** and **Galeries Printemps,** as well as quaint boutique shops like **Au Nain Bleu, Pain d'Ëpices,** or **Si tu Veux**, where you can explore an array of authentic treasures..

Activities at Home

A visit to Disneyland Paris is brief, but you can make the experience last "a little longer" by incorporating surprises and activities before, during, or after the trip, which will add magical memories for the whole family to cherish for longer.

Before the trip, why not plan a special way to reveal the news to the children? Whether it's a gift or a surprise, there are numerous creative options available. You could prepare magical park tickets, arrange for a call from a beloved Disney character (both options available on various online platforms), send a personal letter from Mickey himself, or unveil a secret message written in invisible ink. And it can even be the answer to the final hint on a scavenger hunt!

Another idea to surprise them is to use "fairy dust." There's only one situation in which a mother would voluntarily use powdered glitter at home: this trip. Just be cautious not to let it spread everywhere (or you'll be cleaning glitter "forever"), but it can serve as definitive proof for the children that Tinkerbell has tried to wake them up.

During the trip, you can make a journal with the children to document the best moments of the day. Along with their autograph book, it will help them remember their experiences and become one of their little treasures. And if you have an instant print camera, like a Polaroid, add your photos immediately!

Additionally, while at the park, why not send postcards or letters to family or friends? You can either buy them or create your own, adding a personal touch. As a delightful surprise, consider sending the children a postcard from their favourite character, expressing how much they enjoyed meeting them at Disneyland, or one from Mickey himself, thanking them for their visit. They'll be thrilled to receive such unexpected treasures at home upon their return!

You can buy stamps at hotel receptions and send letters from hotel and park mailboxes (for example, near the Storybook Store and Disney & Co.); postage to Europe and the UK will cost you about €2.

After the trip, why not organise a memory session with movies of their favourite attractions, or a marathon of a particular saga? To ensure the fun isn't just on screen, you can plan an activity related to the movie, such as a craft where you make your own lightsabers, magic wands, or pirate accessories. Build a race track worthy of the Piston Cup or paint the sidewalk with chalk, in the way of Rapunzel— the options are endless!

Another idea to complement this movie session is to cook a "Disney Recipe." There are thousands of websites dedicated to park food or inspired by its characters; you just have to search on Pinterest or Google and you'll find pancakes, waffles, or cupcakes with character shapes or decorations. You can also try making the Frozen milkshake or, if you prefer savoury options, homemade Mickey pizza!

Our favourite recipe, because it's the central element of the story and because of the thousand and one variations you can prepare, is Snow White's caramel apples (although we don't think this count as one of the 5 servings of fruit per day).

In summary, you can take advantage of the time at home to engage in family activities that you will all enjoy, rounding off the most magical trip with your children to Disneyland Paris.

Acknowledgments

To my children Rocío, Jorge, and Cristina, my inspiration, my drive, my luck.

To Manu, this year more than ever, for giving his all for us.

To my parents, the ones that anyone would like to have (and I would like to be).

To my siblings, who let me lean on their shoulders on our trips, in every way. The next thing is for you to let me play my music on the road.

To my family, spread all over the world, but always close. Special thanks to my four grandparents, the best role models of dedication, work, love and life. I carry you in my heart.

To my friends, who celebrate everyone's joys as their own.

To my "editors", who carried me forward and made this guide possible. This version is dedicated to my "translation team", thank you in my most macaronic English.

And, of course, to you, readers, for accompanying me on a magical journey. If you've made it this far, I hope you've had as much fun as I did writing these pages. Your feedback and 'stars' help me reach more families.

Thank you from the bottom of my heart.

CONTACT PHONE NUMBERS AND EMAIL ADDRESSES

Disneyland Paris Booking Office	03448 008 898
Restaurant Booking	+33 (0) 1 60 30 40 50
Guest Relations and Claims	dlp.guest.communication@disneylandparis.com
Photopass information	dlp.photopass@disney.com
Lost Property	Troov App + dlp.objets.trouves@disney.com
VIP Tours	dlp.viptours.experience@disney.com
Special activities	dlp.disney.special.activities@disney.com
	+33 (0) 1 60 30 50 60

English - French Dictionary

English	Francés	English	Francés
Hello	Bonjour	Do you speak English?	Parlez-vous anglais?
Good afternoon	Bonsoir	My name is...	Je m'apelle...
Goodbye	Au revoir	Where is/are...?	Où est...? / Où sont...?
Thank you	Merci	The station	La gare
Please	S'il vous plaît	The bus	Le bus
Yes	Oui	The entrance	L'entrée
No	Non	The hotel	L'hôtel
Excuse me	Excusez-moi	The pharmacy	La pharmacie
You're welcome	De rien	The toilets	Les toilettes
I have a reservation	J'ai réservé	How many of you are there?	Vous êtes combien?
I'm allergic to..	Je suis allérgique aux..	One	Un
I'm a vegan/ a vegetarian	Je suis vegan / végétarien	Two	Deux
How much is it?	Ça fait combien..?	Three	Trois
A water jar	Un carrafe d'eau	Four	Quatre
Can you take a picture of us?	Une photo s'il vous plaît?	Five	Cinq

Land	Attraction	Type	Wait time	Premier Access / Single Rider	EMT	Height and Age Requirements	Pregnancy	Covered
				Disneyland Park				
U.S.A. Main Street	Main Street Vehicles	Slow vehicles	Short wait				Accessible	No
	Horse-Drawn Streetcars	Slow vehicles	Short wait				Accessible	No
	Railroad Station	Slow train ride	Average wait				Accessible	Yes
Fantasyland	Sleeping Beauty Castle	Relaxing walk	No waiting				Accessible	Partly
	Sleeping Beauty Gallery	Relaxing walk	No waiting				Accessible	Yes
	Dragon's Lair	Dark walkthrough attraction	No waiting				Accessible	Yes
	Peter Pan's Flight	Themed dark ride	Very long wait	Premier Access				Yes
	Snow White and the Seven Dwarfs	Themed dark ride	Average wait					Yes
	Les Voyages de Pinocchio	Themed dark ride	Average wait					Yes
	Dumbo the Flying Elephant	Aerial carousel	Long wait		Yes	Not recommended for children under 1 year old	Accessible	No
	Mad Hatter's Tea Cups	Spinning ride	Long wait		Yes		Accessible	Yes
	Alice's Curious Labyrinth	Relaxing walk	No waiting				Accessible	No
	It's a Small World!	Slow boat themed ride	Average wait	Premier Access			Accessible	Yes
	Casey Jr. - Le Petit Train du Cirque	Speedy train ride	Average wait			Not recommended for children under 1 year old	Accessible	No
	Le Pays des Contes de Fées	Slow boat themed ride	Average wait				Accessible	No
	Le Carrousel de Lancelot	Carousel	Average wait		Yes	Babies should ride in one of the two carriages	Accessible	Partly
	Meet Mickey Mouse	Character greeting	Very long wait		Yes		Accessible	Yes
	Princess Pavilion	Character greeting	Very long wait		Yes		Accessible	Yes
Adventureland	Pirates of the Caribbean	Dark ride	Average wait	Premier Access		May frighten younger guests	Accessible	Yes
	Indiana Jones and the Temple of Peril	Roller coaster	Average wait	Premier Access		Minimum height 1.40 m		No
	Pirate's Beach: Skull Rock and Pirate Galleon	Relaxing walk	No waiting				Accessible	No
	Adventure Isle	Relaxing walk	No waiting				Accessible	No
	La Cabane des Robinson	Relaxing walk	No waiting				Accessible	No
	Le Passage Enchanté d'Aladdin	Relaxing walk	No waiting				Accessible	Yes

Land	Attraction	Type	Wait time	Premier Access	EMT	Height and Age Requirements	Pregnancy	Covered
Disneyland Park								
Frontierland	Big Thunder Mountain	Roller coaster	Very long wait	Premier Access	Yes	Minimum height 1.02 m.		No
	Phantom Manor	Dark ride	Long wait	Premier Access		May frighten younger guests		Yes
	Boothill Cemetery	Relaxing walk	No waiting					No
	Rustler Roundup Shootin' Gallery	Shooting gallery	No waiting			Additional fee	Accessible	Yes
	Frontierland Playground	Kids playground	No waiting				Accessible	No
	Thunder Mesa Riverboat Landing	Riverboat ride	Short wait				Accessible	Partly
Discoveryland	Star Wars Hyperspace Mountain	Roller coaster	Very long wait	Premier Access + Single Rider	Yes	Minimum height 1.20 m.		Yes
	Star Tours	3D Motion simulator	Long wait	Premier Access	Yes	Minimum height 1.02 m.		Yes
	Buzz Lightyear Laser Blast	Family adventure	Very long wait	Premier Access	Yes		Accessible	Yes
	Orbitron	Aerial carousel	Average wait	Only Premier Access One	Yes	Not recommended for children under 1 year old		No
	Autopia	Family adventure	Average wait	Premier Access		Minimum height to ride 0.81 m. Minimum height to drive 1.32 m.		No
	Les Mystères du Nautilus	Relaxing walk	Short wait				Accessible	Yes
	Star Port: A Star Wars Encounter	Character greeting	Long wait				Accessible	Yes
Walt Disney Studios								
Worlds of Pixar	Cars Road Trip	Family adventure	Average wait	Premier Access			Accessible	Partly
	Ratatouille: The Adventure	Family adventure	Long wait	Premier Access + Single Rider	Yes			Yes
	Crush's Coaster	Roller coaster	Very long wait	Available + Single Rider queue	Yes	Minimum height 1.07 m.		Yes
	Toy Soldiers Parachutes Drop	Free fall drop tower	Long wait	Single Rider	Yes	Minimum height 0.81 m.		No
	RC Racer	Roller coaster	Average wait	Single Rider	Yes	Minimum height 1.20 m.		No
	Slinky Dog Zigzag Spin	Spinning ride	Short wait		Yes			No
	Cars Quatre Roues Rallye	Speedy vehicle ride	Short wait		Yes			No
Avengers Campus	Avengers Assemble: Flight Force	Roller coaster	Average wait	Premier Access		Minimum height 1.20 m.		Yes
	Spider-Man W.E.B Adventure	Family adventure	Very long wait	Premier Access				Yes
	Hero Training Centre	Character encounter	Long wait			App booking required	Accessible	Yes
	The Twilight Zone Tower of Terror	Free fall drop tower	Very long wait	Premier Access	Yes	Minimum height 1.02 m.		Yes
Toon Studio	Les Tapis Volants - Flying Carpets Over Agrabah	Carousel	Short wait					No
	Animation Academy	Art Masterclass	Average wait				Accessible	Yes

Luggage Checklist I	
Must-haves	**First-Aid kit**
ID's, Passports, Family Record Book + copies	Thermometer
Student identity card / discounts	Pain relievers / antipyretics / anti-inflammatories
European / UK Global Health Insurance Card	Plasters/band-aid's,Compeed blister care, anti-chafing stick
Privale Health insurance card, medical record (if needed)	Chlorhexidine, arnica stick, gauze pads, and saline solution in single-dose packets
Driving license	Sea sickness pills
Insurance documentation	Cold and antihistamine medication, throat lozenges
Phone	Antacid, laxative, antidiarrheal, probiotic, and oral rehydration solution (for children and adults)
Charger (double), power adapted, power bank	Contact lens solution / spare glasses / dental splint
Flight tickets and Hotel reservations	Lip balm
Credit cards (activate international charges)	Hand sanitizer spray or gel
Mastercard (exclusive benefits)	Allergy medication, as prescribed by a doctor
Cash	Wipes and tissues
Travelling with kids to Disneyland Paris guide ;)	Special medication, labelled if it needs to be stored in a fridge
Disneyland Park App, downloaded on your phone	**Backpack (labelled)**
Medical certificates (allergies, disability, pregnancy, priority card, service dogs, pets vaccination)	Water bottle
	Snacks
Phone case with strap / Lanyard	Autograph book and pen
Kids safety bracelets / tags	Entertainment for wait times
Watch / Airtag	Costumes / Mickey ears
Comfortable clothes and shoes	Extra bag for shopping/lockers
Swimsuit and flip - flops	Pins for Pin Trading

Luggage checklist II	
Travelling in bad weather	**Travelling with babies**
Rain cape or poncho, umbrella, waterproof rain jacket	Stroller (labelled and customised)
Waterproof case for documents and phone	Sleeping bag, fleece blanket
Spare shoes, socks and extra clothing	Stroller rain cover
Hats, neck warmers and gloves	Lock
Waterproofing spray	Baby carrier / Sling wrap
Waterproof pants/jackets for kids	Travel picnic blanket, crawling apron
Hand warmer patches or packets	Layered clothing
Travelling in hot weather	Baby food: baby bottles, milk, cereal, baby jars, fruit pouches, spoons...
Sunscreen and aftersun	Silicone or disposable bibs
Sunglasses and hats	Changing mat, diapers, wipes
Refreshing wipes	Toiletry bag
Mosquito repellent, After Bite	Pacifier, comforter, night light
Handheld or stroller fan	Masking tape

Hidden Mickeys

Disneyland Park - Main Street		Disneyland Park - Discoveryland
Disneyland Hotel iron work		Vehicle couplings and cannon at Hyperspace Mountain
Entrance iron work		Buzz Lightyear Laser Blast: as a continent in the map of the planets
Discovery Arcade lamps		Autopia backdrop - Mickey trees
Discovery Arcade moldings		**Walt Disney Studios**
Fences' bollards		Sorcerer's fountain mosaic tiles
Water hydrants		Planters tiles
Orbiton stained glass at the station		Railings and stained glass at the entrance
Disneyland Park - Fantasyland		Disney Junior Dream Factory lamps
Tree grates		Tower of Terror - carried by the little girl
In the stones on Queen of Hearts' Castle		Tower of Terror ceiling lights
Cogs and gears on the "It's a Small World!" facade		"Earful" Tower (Water deposit)
Lancelot Carrousel golden horse		Front Lot Clock
Lancelot Carrousel horse stirrups		Stars in the boarding area of Ratatouille Ride
Old mill barrels		Mater's bonnet (Cars Road Trip)
Disneyland Park - Adventureland		Wheels on Cars Quatre Roue Rallye roof
Pirates of the Caribbean barrels		Studio Photo
Pirates of the Caribbean gold coins and gold plates		Lamp shadow at Flying Carpets
Disneyland Park - Frontierland		Green painted rocks in Toy Story Parachute Drop
Cogs in BTM black locomotive and red locomotive		Brickwork in Stitch Live! queue
Mickey head shaped cacti and barrels		Corals in Crush's Coaster ride
Phantom Manor cobwebs		Mickey and the Magician ironwork railings

Printed in Great Britain
by Amazon

62535216R00107